M000205006

paper books

Voices from Within

Black Poetry from southern Africa

**Introduced and edited by
Michael Chapman and Achmat Dangor**

AD. DONKER / PUBLISHER

AD. DONKER (PTY) LTD
A subsidiary of Donker Holdings (Pty) Ltd
P.O. Box 41021
Craighall
2024

© Michael Chapman and Achmat Dangor 1982

All rights reserved. No part of this publication
may be reproduced, stored in a retrieval system,
or transmitted in any form or by any means, electronic,
mechanical, photocopying, or otherwise, without
the prior permission of the publisher.

First published 1982
First paperbook edition 1986

ISBN 0 86852 119 1

Printed and bound by Creda Press (Pty) Ltd, Cape Town

Contents

6

POST-SOWETO
(1976 —PRESENT DAY)

ANGOLA & MOZAMBIQUE

Introduction

Voices from Within is a comprehensive anthology of black southern African poetry ranging from the earliest known poems of the Khoisan to the apocalyptic Soweto voices of the 1970s. The emphasis falls on poetry from South Africa written in English, but there are also representative examples in translation of traditional and more recent vernacular poetry, translations from the Portuguese of Angolan and Mozambiquan poetry and a selection of poetry from Zimbabwe.

The anthology seeks to convey the extraordinary vitality of black poetry in southern Africa and, by adopting a loose chronological arrangement, to trace a distinctively black-orientated aesthetic development. Fundamental to a black aesthetic is the inextricable relationship which has traditionally existed in African poetry between artistic and social functions: and the poems in this collection stand both as an imaginative and an historically-based record of the Black Experience on a racially turbulent subcontinent.

It seemed justifiable to focus on 'voices within', on those black poets who have continued to write out of a first-hand knowledge of events in southern Africa. This has meant the exclusion of writers such as Mazisi Kunene, Keorapetse Kgositsile, Dennis Brutus and Arthur Nortje, all of whom either chose or were forced into exile before they had established themselves as poets in southern Africa itself. But these and more recent writers-in-exile have received extensive coverage in Afro-American and general African anthologies, as well as in collections which have concentrated specifically on the poetry of exiled South Africans.

It also seemed right to include translated poems. While certain aesthetic qualities will obviously be lost in translation, the forcefulness and relevance of the 'messages' continue to make an impact, and convey further manifestations of that central theme of oppression and liberation. It is not really surprising that black poetry, whether from the past or the present, whether from South Africa, Zimbabwe, Angola or Mozambique, should display larger coherences. This poetry as a whole has more often than not been written in direct reaction to the kind of racial stereotypes foisted on blacks by the colonial mentality. Black southern African poetry has generally had to affirm the black man's need for self-identification, for re-establishing images, myths and modes of perception arrived at in the first instance from the experience of his Blackness.

Further, by including translations especially of vernacular poetry, *Voices from Within* is able to indicate some of the fascinating parallels between traditional African literary approaches and modern strategies. The section on Traditional Poetry includes prayers, hymns, fables, laments and praise poems; and most of these forms reappear, dictated by new social conditions, in the work of contemporary poets. One may, for example, compare the traditional Sotho 'Lament for a Warrior' with Oswald Mtshali's politically-motivated 'Weep Not for a Warrior'. Or one may examine the way in which traditional mythological references have, in a number of poems today, been translated into the mythological figures of a new South African landscape, one where bulldozers metamorphosed into mad beasts raze shacks and so dictate mechanical policies of 'resettlement'. Also, similar motifs will be found to have occurred in earlier and more recent poetry. The motif of mother and child, for instance, has at different times been imbued with both religious and social resonances; it has thus been made to suggest both the African cosmological concept of the unity of being as well as the ideal alternative to contemporary socio-political problems of family disintegration. This is apparent in Sipho Sepamla's 'Song of Mother and Child', a traditional African lullaby re-imagined within a context of migrant labour on the gold-mines.

In addition contemporary poets, in their attempts to reach a black communal audience, have found particularly conducive to literary creation many of the organising principles of traditional oral poetry, including its context of performance. Both Ingoapele Madingoane's 'black trial' and Mothobi Mutloatse's 'Ngwana wa

Azania' (a 'proemdra' in which 'prose, poem and drama are one') elevate improvisation, the 'destruction of the text', above a Western, Platonic sense of ideal form. Just as the traditional praise poem was a vehicle of both praise and criticism, so S.E.K. Mqhayi, in his 'modern' praise poem 'The Prince of Britain', was during the Royal Visit of 1925 able to hymn George VI at the same time as he commented unfavourably on British Imperial designs. Just as the imbongi, or praise poet, effectively employed devices of repetition, parallelism and ideophones, so Mongane Serote makes striking use of such rhetorical means in his highly contemporary epic, 'No Baby Must Weep', wherein the personal-lyrical 'I' assumes a communal-historical dimension. A traditional praise poem such as 'Praises of the King Tshaka' characteristically employed a hyperbolic 'boasting' imagery and the device of naming; and we find similar techniques featuring in the work of contemporary poets such as Serote, Mtshali and Christopher van Wyk. In Van Wyk's 'About Grafitti', for instance, the paraphernalia of township life are urgently 'named' in order to overwhelm the listener with the sense of an accumulated black presence rising from the very gutters to which apartheid would consign it.

As the divisions of this anthology suggest, the cataclysmic events of Sharpeville (1960) and Soweto (1976) have been watersheds in black South African literature. With publishing opportunities for blacks severely limited, black poetry prior to Sharpeville appeared mainly in newspapers such as *Ilanga Lase Natal* and was distinguished by a struggle on the part of the poet writing in English to free himself from mission-school and Western humanist influences which were often debilitating because unapt under the circumstances. It is true that a mission-school idiom is impressively utilised in 'Santa Cruz: The Holy Cross' (1898) by A.K. Soga, who has been rightly described by Tim Couzens in his doctoral study, *The New African,* as the 'first really serious black South African poet writing in English'. But by the 1930s and forties black poets, no longer subscribing to the Christian optimism that had characterised earlier black writing, were becoming increasingly aware of the need to find forms specifically dictated by modern South African socio-political dilemmas.

Writing against a background of job reservation (L.R's ' "Civilised" Labour Policy'), the Sophiatown squatter movement of the 1940s ('Shantytown') and English-speaking South African liberalism's failure to accommodate rising black nationalist expectations (Dhlomo's 'Valley of a Thousand Hills'), poets such as Peter

Abrahams and H.I.E. Dhlomo, in particular, deliberately turned away from those mainstream Western literary models sanctioned by a liberal tradition. Instead Abrahams, during the thirties, sought a valid idiom of protest in the harsh Afro-American poetry of, amongst others, Langston Hughes. Dhlomo for his part rejected a Western-inspired individualism in favour of a communal ethic, while analytic modes gave way to 'rhythm', synthesis, as the essence of Blackness (concepts central too to Dhlomo's Negritude contemporaries, including Leopold Senghor). Abrahams's tough, Americanised diction and Dhlomo's African humanism, with its reverence for family and its principles of communalism, have since become important features of a new post-Sharpeville black South African poetry, a poetry whose distinctive stylistic sensibility has increasingly been designated by the acronym 'Soweto'.

Soweto poetry — or, as it has also been called, the New Black poetry, or People's or Participatory poetry — began to appear in the mid-1960s, after the almost total proscription of a previous generation of Sophiatown prose writing. This poetry, in the first work of Casey Motsisi, Njabulo Ndebele, Mtshali, Serote and Mafika Gwala, concentrated on the immediacy of day-to-day life in Soweto itself. And Soweto as a social and metaphysical entity has continued to provide the stimulus for a poetry which has generally adopted a stark English idiom and a ghetto-derived imagery, and which has eschewed rhyme and closed forms in favour of open or 'naked' forms. These stylistic features have proved to be utterly appropriate to the rigours of contemporary black South African experience.

The intellectual and literary background to Soweto poetry emphasises a radically altered sense of reality in South Africa since Sharpeville. A failure of African National Congress post-war multiracial ideals (see Dhlomo's embittered 'Not for Me'), a rejection by blacks of the more patronising forms of English-speaking South African liberalism, an acceptance instead of their group identity, of the importance of power and of a literature of commitment whose central metaphor is change — these are the salient features of a poetry which, having been given prominence by a growing South African publishing industry, has during the 1970s vigorously insisted on its own terms of reference.

These New Black poets inevitably have not had quite the same problem earlier black South African writers had of having to confront often inappropriate Eurocentric literary influences. Ironically, this is largely because over twenty years of Bantu

Education (a policy of basic vernacular instruction in a modern economy) have virtually robbed the present-day black generation of a facility in the English language and as a result in English, including Afro-English, literary traditions. (In addition, many works by black writers which might have offered relevant examples are currently banned in South Africa.) Yet, despite this, the creative imagination — as it has always done — has turned obstacles to its own advantage. In the case of Soweto poetry, it has forged a literary sensibility free of any obviously imported models and excitingly attuned to Black Consciousness ideals of social and psychological transformation. Such ideals were tellingly propounded by the South African Students Organisation (SASO) before it was banned in 1977, and had by the early mid-seventies won widespread acceptance among South African urban blacks, particularly the youth.

Initially Soweto poetry was directed in protest at a predominantly white 'liberal' readership. By the time of the Soweto disturbances in 1976, however, the emphasis had shifted with the Black Consciousness voices particularly of Serote ('No Baby Must Weep') and Gwala ('Getting off the Ride') finding their full power in an uncompromising poetry of resistance — a mobilising rhetoric imparting to a black audience a message of consciousness-raising and race-pride.

Whereas early Soweto poetry, as it appeared in Mtshali's seminal volume *Sounds of a Cowhide Drum* (1971), may be described in familiar humanist terms as offering an 'interpretation' of a pre-existent reality, the later poetry has been aptly described by Es'kia Mphahlele, in his review of Mtshali's banned *Fireflames* collection* (1980), as having assumed a 'hard apocalyptic tone'. The voice which one encounters in the more recent poetry of Mtshali, Serote, Gwala, Madingoane, Van Wyk and Fhazel Johennesse accepts the implications of an historically-conditioned not an eternal nature, and thus prophesies change. Whereas the first Soweto poetry took as its highest ideal the Western one of justice, the poetry which has emerged since June '76, and which has found an outlet in *Staffrider* magazine, has rediscovered the African ideal of heroism. This 'Post-Soweto' poetry has more and more begun to focus not so much backwards on the horrors of the township streets as forward to a revolutionary future.

The same broad shift of direction — from protest to liberating vision — is apparent too in the poems presented here from Angola, Mozambique and Zimbabwe. In fact, Musaemura Zimunya's
* recently unbanned.

description of the poetry 'inspired by the struggle for Zimbabwe' is pertinent to contemporary southern African poetry as a whole:

> It is a communion of voices, surging forward like Musiwatunya (the 'Victoria Falls') and they compel our audience and attention — compel us, that is, by their unity of imagination and purpose, once and for all defying enslavement and imprisonment, death and destruction, bombs and bullets . . . This is the voice of Liberation. In community, we have the makings of a movement here.
>
> (Commendation, *And Now the Poets Speak,* 1981)

Voices from Within gives vivid expression to just such a poetry which has found both sociological and artistic value in the close relation of literature, southern African specifics and the participatory ideals of black community.

In preparing this anthology, we wish to thank Dr. Tim Couzens of the African Studies Institute, University of the Witwatersrand, for making his research on early black literature available to us, as well as *Staffrider* magazine where a number of poems collected here first appeared. We have also drawn on biographical information compiled by the National English Literary Museum and Documentation Centre, Grahamstown.

M.C.
A.D.
1982

Traditional

San ('Bushman')

Prayer to the Hunting Star, Canopus
said by X-nanni

Xkoagu, give me your heart
that you sit with in plenty.
Take my heart, my heart
small and famished without hope
so that like you I too may be full
    for I hunger.

You seem to me full-bellied, Xkoagu
and in my eyes not small
    but I am hungry.

Star, give to me your belly
that fills you with a good feeling,
and you shall take my stomach from me
so you as well can know its hunger.
Give me your right arm too
and you shall take my arm from me,
my arm that does not kill
    for I miss my aim.

Xkoagu, blind with your light
    the Springbok's eyes,
and you shall give me your arm
for my arm that hangs here
that makes me miss my mark.

The Wind and the Bird

(Naron Bushman Song)

The Wind is a man and goes out from his hut.
As a bird, Xgauwa goes with the Wind:
one with two names are they, Xgauwa and Hise.
The Wind has the bird with him and he walks a little way
but no more: from the earth he rises,
into the sky he shoots up, he soars
and he takes the grass and whirls it far
scatters it so it falls a great distance.
The magician sees the one walking with the Wind,
it is Xgauwa, and the bird speaks to him saying,
'I am he who arouses the Wind.'

Recited by the San X-nanni to W.H.I. Bleek in 1885
and recorded and interpreted by him.

Khoi-Khoi ('Hottentot')

Hymn to Tsui-Xgoa*

You, O Tsui-Xgoa
you, all-father
you, our father!
Let stream to earth the thundercloud,
give that our flocks may live,
give life to us.
I am so stricken with weakness
I thirst and I hunger.
Allow that I gather and eat the field fruits,
for are you not our first one
the father of fathers,
you, Tsui-Xgoa —
that we may sing to you in praise
that we may measure to you in return,
you, all-father
you, our maker
you, O Tsui-Xgoa.

* Supreme Being

How Death Came

The Moon, they say, called Mantis,
sent him with life to people saying:
Go to men and tell them this —
    As I die and dying live,
    you too shall die and dying live.
Mantis started, took the word.
Then Hare stopped him by the path,
he said: What, insect, is your errand?
Mantis answered: I am sent by Moon,
by that one, I must say to men —
    As he dies and dying lives
    they too shall die and dying live.
Hare the quick-tongue said to him:
Why run? You are shaky on your legs.
Let me go, I outrun the wind.
Hare ran, he came to men and said:
Moon sent me with this word —
    As I die and dying perish
    you shall die and utterly die.
Hare raced again to Moon,
told him all that he had said to men.
The Moon said dark with anger:

How is it you dared tell them
this thing I never said?
He took up wood, a sharp fire-log,
with one blow in the face
struck down the Hare. He split
the lying Hare's lip to this day.

*From the MSS of Hottentot folklore in the
original language in the Grey Collection,
Cape Town, quoted by W.H.I. Bleek in
Hottentot Fables and Tales, 1864

Sotho

Lament for a Warrior

Sister of the Dead
Women, if we held the oxhide shield
and I had stood by him in battle
he would have come, my mother's son,
he would not have died, our child,
but walking home have said: I fell
only when I tripped up on a stone.

Chorus of Women
Ao! has he gone has he gone
and left us here alone?
Tell us, has his soul been sent
never to see us again,
and all of them, all gone
where there's no returning?
Will the earth's womb not be filled,
will the grave have never done!

Zulu

Praises of the King Tshaka

He thinks of war
Son of the righteous one, he who thunders on the ground,
bird, devourer of other birds,
great leaper who bounds over all others —
the hill on whose sides are no grazing cattle,
where the antelopes browse in herds,
the waterbuck feed and the crawling thousand-legs.
Red paradise flycatcher
as if with a head that is dust-covered,
he is making sport of the Swazi King Sobhuza.

He overwhelms the King Zwide
He is the stealthy leopard and for long
he has blocked the river crossings against the rabble,
blocking the way against Ngobe of Zwide's family
who had to go over by the drift at which females cross.
He is the river ford with the slippery stepping-stones
and they slipped on the stones, Zwide and his son.
A wild beast, he rose from the thickets in anger against
    the people.
Storm thundering down on the town of Kugoba,
he bore off the shields of their Amaphela regiment.
The calf mounted to the house of Zwide's mother
while the others said it was madness.
He felled Nomahlanyana born to the king Zwide,
he slaughtered Sikhunyana born to Zwide,
he felled Nqabeni and Mphepha,
He ate up Dayingubo born to Zwide.
Ceaselessly he pursued the man.
I wondered at him chasing the son of Langa
forcing him to the sun's rising
and then following him into the West.

Tshaka takes advice
Old men forever rail against the young,
but I shall listen to the tale of an old woman,
one whom I find alone in the ragged corn gardens.
And I shall hear the tale of an old man
whom I find alone along the trail.

The women mock him
He was the joke of the women of Zululand,
they joked while they sat in his celibate hut
saying that Tshaka never would rule,
that it was not his to be King.

And indeed it was in the year he began to live in
   comfort.

He punishes treachery
Uzihlandhlo and Gcwele are wizards
showing him instead that which still ran with blood.
The people of Majola were annihilated
and a heap of bones are the children of Tayi
who had lain ready in ambush;
even this day the ridge of Tayi's children stands
   amazed.

He is foiled by Moshesh
The locust was caught in the shift of the assegais
   among the ancient tribe of Mlandela,
and when it flew up it travelled far.
He scaled up to the heights of Mbozane
and there the dancers for him were a line of grey
   antelopes
and a rooster started up and blocked his way.

Tshaka wearies of killing
The buffalo stands at bay on the great river
and the Pondos tremble to descend on it.
He went out and seized the cattle of Faku in Pondoland;
he seized those of Gambushe in Pondoland;
he took those of the Basuto, the blanketed ones,
and those of the Baca who wear fringed hair.
Ungengi, cease from killing the enemy, it is Summer
and your feet will be entangled in the grass.
Tshaka is not to be spat out, nor is he like water.

His name is fear
I saw the grey hawk swoop like a bolt on the cattle
   of Macingwana,
the blazing fire of Mjokwane's son,
the devastating rush of fire
that burnt out the Buthelezi like owls.
Tshaka! I fear to speak the name Tshaka!
For Tshaka was king of the people of Mashobane.
Raving mad he ravened among the towns
and until dawn came the towns called to each other.
He seized firmly the assegais of his father,
he who was like the maned lion.

Ngoni Burial Song

The earth does not ever grow fat
it swallows the head-plumed fighters
and we shall fall to the earth — Nhi hi hi!
The earth does not ever grow fat
it swallows up the swift-acting heroes
and shall we die, we too? — Nhi hi hi!

Listen, Earth! Do you wish to make us mourn?
Listen, Earth! Shall all of us die? — Nhi hi hi!

The earth does not ever grow fat,
it makes an end of the kings
and we shall fall to the earth — Nhi hi hi!

The earth does not ever grow fat,
it swallows as well all the hearts
and shall we die, we too? — Nhi hi hi!

Listen, O you who sleep, wrapped close in the grave,
shall we all go down in the ground? Ho ho ho ho!
Listen, O World, for the sun is setting now,
    we all shall enter the earth.

Love is Bitter

Age grips the body but the heart stays young,
The wooden bowl wears through with many meals,
No tree-trunk in its age can keep its bark,
No lover rests but that his rival weeps.

Pre-Sharpeville
(1890 – 1960)

A.K. Soga

Ntsikana's Vision

What 'thing', Ntsikana, was't that prompted thee
To preach to thy dark countrymen beneath thy tree?
What sacred vision did that mind enthral
Whilst thou lay dormant in thy cattle kraal?

Was it the sun, uprising in his pride,
That struck with glittering sheen Hulushe's dappled side,
By Chumie's laughing fountain hastening merrily,
To meet strong Keisi's waters rolling to the sea?

A Vision? Yea! That presence once had shone
Upon the man of Tarshish, down from the heavenly throne,
And in the holy light of His mysterious Word
The proud Barbarian bows and worships God, the Lord!

Hark! 'Tis the sound of prayer, of savage melody —
Untutored voices raised to Him who sits on high;
Those hills and dales around fair Gwali's stream
Repeat again Ntsikana's sacred Hymn!

Wake, Gaika, wake! I see the gathering storm
By Debe's plains; Gcaleka's horse and Ndlambe's legions swarm;
Behold thy tribesmen scattered, thy warriors' doom is sealed —
The word of God rejected — by prophecy revealed.

(1897)

Santa Cruz : The Holy Cross

The Cross; a symbol of that faith,
    That points to Calvary;
A living token of that Death
    That sets the guilty free.

Long hath it stood, so silently,
    Where Algoa's rock-bound shore
Beats back the waters of the sea
    With angry sullen roar.

It tells of man's belief in God;
    Of Diaz and his band,
Who braved the waters and the flood,
    At Christian King's command.

It speaks of Freedom's flag unfurled,
　　For Christianity;
A beacon light, in this dark world,
　　To God and liberty.

On Santa Cruz, long may it stand,
　　As emblem, may it be
The cheer of Good Hope; in the land
　　Peace and prosperity.

Rev. Pambani Jeremiah Mzimba

It Walks

But to me it is clear
that even the Black man in Africa must stand
on his feet in matters of worship like
people in other countries, and not
always expect to be carried by the
White man on his back. He has long
learnt to walk by leaning on the
White man, but today he must stand
without leaning on anybody except
his God so that the work of the
Gospel should flourish . . . The child
itself feels it must walk, it
stumbles and falls, takes one step
at a time, but the end result is
that it walks.

(1898)

J.I. Msikinya

Africa's Tears

Come to me, oh, ye children
For I am old and out of date;
Bring with you the wisdom
Whence it may be obtained;
Tell me not of Socrates and Plato
For their words are old and grey,
But your youngest infant State.

I have worried long without you
For a thousand years or so
Come and put us 'in the know';
I have sat in the quiet cloister
My light behind a bush,
And I need your kind assistance
In the modern game of push.
                    (1904)

Mrs. A.C. Dube

Africa: My Native Land

How beautiful are thy hills and thy dales!
I love thy very atmosphere so sweet,
Thy trees adorn the landscape rough and steep
No other country in the whole world could with thee compare.

It is here where our noble ancestors
Experienced joys of dear ones and of homes;
Where great and glorious kingdoms rose and fell,
Where blood was shed to save thee, thou dearest
     land ever known.

But, alas! Their efforts were all in vain
For today others claim thee as their own
No longer can their offspring cherish thee,
No land to call their own — but outcasts in their
     own country.

Despair of thee I never, never will,
Struggle I must for freedom — God's great gift —
Till every drop of blood within my veins
Shall dry upon my troubled bones, oh thou Dearest
     Native Land.

(1913)

S.E.K. Mqhayi

The Prince of Britain
Translated from the Xhosa

Body-That-Smokes is the name I greet you by;
Burning-Body is your pet name;
Scourge-of-the-Nation you are called in private;
The praise-singer calls you Flasher-of-Lightning;
    Honour to you!

Go out, all of you, go out and identify him.
Go out, all the nations, and identify.
What kind of creature is this unknown monster?
Never before seen, unfamiliar to all?
Perhaps he may turn out to be Nabulele,
Monster of the deep pools.
Or Makhanda-mahlanu, the snake with five heads, who
    comes as a whirlwind.

Or Gilikankqo,
The monster whose lair no man knows.
Its body smokes like fire,
Its body burns like flame.
It spits sparks as if it were a steam-engine.
It flashes lightning like the heavens.
    Honour to you!

Here comes the Prince of Britain!
Offspring of the female buffalo, Victoria! —
Young woman who is a god in the land of the blacks.
Spirit-like, priest of war, wizard,
Here comes the boy son of George V;
Of the Royal House, a boy coming to men.
Dung-coloured one whose eye flashes lightning.
If it so much as touches you with a glance, it will blind you.
The dung-coloured one, who is a — it's impossible to tell
    by looking at him —
His eyes are like living creatures when they look at you.

There is no-one can gaze at the calf of the wild beast —
And those who once tried collapsed unconscious.
Here comes the boy of the raw dung, the old dung of
    royal descent.
Here he comes in plumes and in feathers.
Here he comes decked in finery, wearing the grass of the
    initiates.
Here he comes beautifully attired, resplendent and
    bejewelled.

Here he comes in scent and fragrance, in mint and grass
    necklaces
        smelling of the sacred tambuti
Here he comes with the virtue of the leopard, the lion,
Here he comes in raiment and fine robes.
    Honour to you,
                            Philistine indeed!

Hail, Great Britain!
Great Britain on whom the sun never sets;
What shall we do with this princely child?
What shall we do with this child of the king?
Give answer, you mountains of our land.
And you, rivers of our home, speak out!
Bring him down, waves of the sea!
Waves of the sea, bring him down,
So that we may see him and study him intently.

A shooting star once came here:
Could it be that he is on its trail?
It came to the people of Phalo, son of Tshiwo,
To the Zulus, the Sothos, the Swazi, the Tswana;
It was a pilgrim to the brotherhood of the Blacks.
For Jehovah, the Lord, ruleth —
He speaks of His creation.
He hastens on His times.

Hail, light that shines,
Have you come to fetch your star?
We are a nation that divides stars amongst us.
Yonder is the morning star — star of your people.
But we bind ourselves together with the stars of June,
    month of ploughing,
The stars we count our years by, the years of our manhood.

Hayi, the mighty Great Britain!
Here she comes with bible and bottle,
Here she comes, a missionary escorted by a soldier,
    with gun powder and guns,
    with cannons and breechloader.
Forgive me, O Father, but which of these must we accept?
Pass on, calf of the beast,
Trampler who even now is trampling,
Pass on and return safely — eater of our country's inheritance.
Long live the king!
I've said enough about him, I'll say no more,
Like the shooting star we once saw.

                            (1925)

D.G.T. Bereng

The Birth of Moshesh
Translated from the Sotho

What began that bustle in the village,
Why all the stirring in the yards?
What moves the restless women from hut to hut
Or has the young men glancing round?
What sets menfolk at each other's ears,
Of what dread things do the drums speak;
What starts the hollow bull horns booming,
Strums on the sounding calabash strings
And what reed notes these in the shrill pipes?
See now the smiling women's faces,
All the young men amazed,
And the elders speaking in tough riddles.

Bright and clear the veld,
Echoes ringing in the hills,
And the sound hung above the peaks
And all the cliff caves rebounding.
The wild beasts roamed uneasily
And the antelopes went skipping away;
The animals went unheeded in this daze of news
And men and women left wondering:

To Libenyane a man-child is born.
He emerged with a shield gripped in his hand.
In his face the people read great deeds
Heralded before they came to be;
And things were dark to ponder.
For men saw plants grow as they watched
And flowers bloom luxuriant,
Stars streamed in the day sky
Like midnight lightnings.

They saw flame-tongues in the sun
And in their huts men laid aside their blankets.
The moon stood still against the sky
Like a shy bride before her husband's father.
Through a cranny the whispering was heard,
The cattle also seemed to listen
And soon their lowing was loud;
The wet-nosed household gods bellowing out,
Lions roaring in the plains
Roar and give way before the King.
Leopards roaring in the krantzes
Roar and give way before the King.

The wild beasts made the world tremble
For him, Moshesh, though but an infant,
Man-child suckled on the milk of antelopes.

Thus and thus we knew Thesele was born
For when born, he Letlama, a son of Mokhachane,
The day the great Lepoqo saw the light
We sang new songs unknown to us
And for us the young girls swung in dance.
Then it was we could say:
Halala! You Zulu of Natal!
We too have a true chief today.
And you on Caledon's banks, see our pride!
We too raise battle shields today;
We stand free at the rock fastness, Thaba Bosio.
Stronghold given by God to Thesele.

L.R.

'Civilised' Labour Policy

Hertzog is my shepherd; I am in want.
He maketh me to lie down on park benches.
He leadeth me beside still factories.
He arouseth my doubt of his intention.
He leadeth me in the path of destruction for his Party's sake.
Yea, I walk through the valley of the shadow of destruction
And I fear evil, for thou art with me,
The Politicians and the Profiteers, they frighten me,
Thou preparest a reduction in my salary before me,
In the presence of mine enemies.
Thou anointest mine income with taxes,
My expense runneth over.
Surely unemployment and poverty will follow me
All the days of this Administration
And I shall dwell in a mortgaged house forever.

(1932)

J.J.R. Jolobe

The Making of a Servant
Translated from the Xhosa

I can no longer ask how it feels
To be choked by a yoke-rope
Because I have seen it for myself in the chained ox.
The blindness has left my eyes. I have become aware,
I have seen the making of a servant
In the young yoke-ox.

He was sleek, lovely, born for freedom,
Not asking anything from anyone, simply
        priding himself on being a young ox.
Someone said: Let him be caught and
        trained and broken in,
Going about it as if he meant to help him.
I have seen the making of a servant
In the young yoke-ox.

He tried to resist, fighting for his freedom.
He was surrounded, fenced in with wisdom and experience.
They overcame him by trickery: 'He must be trained.'
A good piece of rationalisation can camouflage evil.
I have seen the making of a servant
In the young yoke-ox.

He was bound with ropes that cut into his head,
He was bullied, kicked, now and again petted,
But their aim was the same: to put a yoke on him.
Being trained in one's own interests is for the privileged.
I have seen the making of a servant
In the young yoke-ox.

The last stage. The yoke is set on him.
They tie the halter round his neck, slightly choking him.
They say the job's done, he'll be put to work with
        the others
To obey the will of his power and taskmaster.
I have seen the making of a servant
In the young yoke-ox.

He kicks out, trying to break away.
They speak with their whips. He turns backwards
Doing his best to resist but then they say: 'Hit him.'
A prisoner is a coward's plaything.
I have seen the making of a servant
In the young yoke-ox.

Though he stumbled and fell, he was bitten on the tail.
Sometimes I saw him raking at his yoke-mate
With his horns — his friend of a minute, his blood-brother.
The suffering under the yoke makes for bad blood.
I have seen the making of a servant
In the young yoke-ox.

The sky seemed black as soft rain fell.
I looked at his hump, it was red,
Dripping blood, the mark of resistance.
He yearns for his home, where he was free.
I have seen the making of a servant
In the young yoke-ox.

Stockstill, tired, there was no sympathy.
He bellowed notes of bitterness.
They loosened his halter a little — to let him breathe,
They tightened it again, snatching back his breath.
I have seen the making of a servant
In the young yoke-ox.

I saw him later, broken, trained.
Pulling a double-shared plough through deep soil,
Serving, struggling for breath, in pain.
To be driven is death. Life is doing things for yourself.
I have seen the making of a servant
In the young yoke-ox.

I saw him climb the steepest of roads.
He carried heavy loads, staggering —
The mud of sweat which wins profit for another.
The savour of working is a share in the harvest.
I have seen the making of a servant
In the young yoke-ox.

I saw him hungry with toil and sweat,
Eyes all tears, spirit crushed.
No longer able to resist. He was tame.
Hope lies in action aimed at freedom.
I have seen the making of a servant
In the young yoke-ox.

M.G.

Black and White

To be so black is curse you say,
For God has deigned it so;
A greater lie ne'er came man's way,
To toss him to and fro.

The blackness of the changing night,
Is part of shining day,
For God did make creation right.
With black and white to stay.

Walter M.B. Nhlapo

The Revolution Song

This revolution song travels wide
'Tis constant as the flowing tide —
A murmuring distinct to all
Whose ears will listen to the call.
Hark, hear the strain, the melody,
It fills the listeners with glee,
It causes faint hearts to grow strong
And lend their voices to the throng.
So join the tune, ye black folk;
Someday 'twill remove the yoke.
O, chant it loud, you dusky braves,
Sing of the day your spirit craves.
Mix concrete and make roads, but softly croon,
On ancient talkin' drums beat loud the tune;
Go forth uniting every heart
In links no foe can ever part.
Go across the deserts and the sea,
And sing, 'Blackmen shall be free!'
Go everywhere beneath the sun,
Join all black souls into one.

                        (1936)

Tomorrow

Not with the moans of a damn slave
Shall my song resound:
Like white folks freedom I'll have,
And shall fly over the earth.

Not as a scorned 'Kaffir boy',
Continually kicked in life.
But free, heart full of joy
Shall my song then be.

                (1950)

S.C. Faber

The Scolly

His hair is woolly, his face is brown,
    His glance is furtive, his smile a sneer,
The backstreet hero of every town,
    The bully and the buccaneer!
He is the stepson of our nation,
    A menace to future bliss,
The product of civilisation,
    The scollyboy disturbing peace!
Get off the pavement as he staggers,
    And as by night he comes to life
He uses razors, or a dagger,
    Or in your side he sticks a knife!
When he is caught you never waver,
    You whip him as he burns with hate;
An oath escapes him, not a prayer,
    He knows that it is too late
Too late to change his mode of living,
    Or to forgive the human beings,
The dirty streets, the vice, the thieving
    Through hunger for a million things!
And as he stands defiant, foul,
    A man without God or shame,
Just listen to your own soul
    And hear him whisper — 'You're to blame!'

B.W. Vilakazi

I Hear a Singing
Translated from the Zulu

When first I heard our tribal songs
They seemed to me of little worth;
But now their message echoes in my heart.
Secrets and timeless passions haunt a lilt
Inspired by Zululand's sons and their traditions.
These songs recall a past so swiftly fading
That now I fear its meaning may elude me
Although I weep with longing to preseve it.
The songs that you, O children of Ngungunyana,
O Vendas of Thobela, have perfected —
Sung through the years by fathers of our fathers
Whose huts were large and strongly built,
Whose pipes were horns of ox or buffalo,
Whose women chattered underneath the trees —
Torment my soul with eagerness to match them.

The Gold Mines
Translated from the Zulu

Roar and clang, you machines of the mines,
Roar from dawn till darkness falls;
I shall wake, O let me be!
Roar, machines, continue deaf
To black men groaning as they labour
Tortured by their aching muscles,
Gasping in the fetid air,
Reeking from the dirt and sweat,
Shaking their bodies desperately.

Bellow you frenzied bulls of steel!
Far is that place where first you came to life
And — roasted by fiery furnaces
Until you were ready and only ash remained —
Were quickly dispatched, and having crossed the sea
Were loaded on trucks, for puffing fuming engines
To bring you to Goli, place of gold, and us.
Loudly you bellowed, till we, like frightened dassies
Swarming towards you, answered your strident summons.

These dassies, each and all, were black,
And, shorn of their tails, you captured them;
Then you pushed them down the mine,
Exploited them and drained their strength.
Turn you tireless wheels of steel!
I know you did not choose to come
And cause us all this drudgery.
For you no less enslaved, must toil and roar
Till, one by one, worn out you rot
On some neglected rubbish plot.

Sometimes, as I walk along the road,
I turn to look at you and wonder
If you as well beget each other,
Increase and multiply! — How vain a thought!
Yet we are brothers, for we like you, must rot,
Be shattered and exploited in the mines
Until, with damaged lungs and ebbing strength
We cough without relief, collapse and die.
But you are spared that fatal coughing — Why?

Around the noisy compounds of the mines,
We hear that black men born of many tribes
Had come to raise these great white dumps,
Astounding to their ancestors.
Yes, when a siren screeched one day
A poor black dassie heard its call
And answering its summons, in confusion
Was trapped, and then, transformed into a mole,
Was forced to burrow deep and search for gold.

Soon swarms of puzzled dassies came to join it:
Then swiftly rose the great white dumps:
Deep were the holes and high the hills —
Sandlwana itself is now no higher!
Sweating I climb them, reach the top
And watch the dust like clouds of smoke
I see them swirling there beneath me
Forever obscuring the sullied earth.

Roar and clang, you machines of the mines!
Thunder loudly and louder yet.
Drown our voices with your clamour,
Stifle our cries and groans of pain
The while you eat away our joints.
Mock us, old tyrants, callous and mighty.
Let our suffering cause your laughter!
Too well we know your terrible powers,
For you are the masters — we the slaves!

When we agreed to leave our huts
Be herded like oxen, forget we are men,
We left our mealies and creamy milk
To eat this lumpy, soggy porridge.
Our manhood diminished and known as 'boys'
We all must acknowledge our world has changed;
Now, wakened at dawn, we stand in lines,
Thinking — how strange to be interred,
Open-eyed creatures buried alive!

Roar, as you will, machines of the mines!
I am awake and never dawdle;
See I am going underground
To shatter the rock-face with my pick;
And you above, though hearing nothing,
Will know I wield the white man's drill
Because you see the little trolleys
Filled with stones of white and green.

My brother also carries a pick
Heaves a spade upon his shoulder,
Drags on his feet a miner's boots
And enters the shaft to follow me.
The earth soon swallows us who burrow,
And, if I perish underground,
What does it matter, who am I?
Day after day, O, fellow men! —
I, helpless, watch my brother collapse.

Where I have come from, far away,
The lands are free of towering buildings
Whose tops I stretch my neck to see;
But when I return there, clutching my bundle,
All I can find are shrivelled stalks
And empty huts; I scratch my head
And ask about my family.
They answer:'Ask your white employer!' —
I close my mouth in weary silence.

Roar, still louder, machines of the mines!
Though far away in Germiston.
Your clamour penetrates my soul
And echoes in my ears
Like distant bells of booming brass;
They bring to mind the giant buildings
Owned by men enriched by me
Who daily exploit my sweated toil,
While I, the proverbial church mouse, starve.

Yet, thunder more softly, you harsh machines!
Because the white man's heart is stone,
Must you be pitiless too, O steel?
Silence your uproar in the mines
And listen I beg you to all our pleas,
Or else we too may have no pity
When, on that day the future hides,
We cry at last: 'O things of iron,
You are the slaves of black men now!'

Beware! Though now my hands are empty,
These puny arms, in days gone by,
Wielded the fatal assagais,
Which as we hurled them, darkened the earth.
Great Queen Victoria's realm was shaken,
Paul Kruger's soldiers terrified —
And yet we were defeated!
But still I dream — O steel contraptions! —
That lands our fathers once possessed
Shall, by their sons be ruled again.

Today I have no place to rest
Beneath dark clouds of alien power;
Our fathers' fields lie barren now,
Untilled by men all cowed like me.
For even if I owned great wealth,
This land my father's fathers owned,
I never may purchase or possess.
O, mighty spirits of heaven and earth! —
Will you not end this vile oppression?

Down in our fathers' resting place
Where you, our ancestral spirits dwell,
They say your powers are unsurpassed
When you commune with God
Who sees the man - but not his colour! —
Here, earth is reddened with my blood
That clots and dries in savage heat
While I, exhausted, pray to you —
But hear no echo in reply.

O see how day by day this land
Is being plundered by those who seized it —
These foreigners who enrich themselves
While I and my deprived black brothers
Are landless, penniless, empty-handed!
Above the mine-pits grass is green,
Vivid as heaven's blest horizon,
Where dwell the spirits to whom we pray —
But they, alas, are silent still!

How loud your roar, machines of the mines!
My hands are torn,
My feet are swollen,
They throb, but where are remedies? —
White men's medicines cost much money!
Hush, you machines, and spare my ears!
Well have I served my rich white masters, —
But O my soul is heavy within me!

Subdue your thunder! I long to sleep,
Close tight my eyes, hear nothing more,
And dread no longer tomorrow's dawn.
I yearn to sleep and wake afar
Where I may know among the spirits,
Repose unmarred by earthly turmoil,
When I, enwrapped by ancestral arms,
Shall rest at last in heaven's own green pastures.

Peter Abrahams

Self

I am a shadow,
Restless,
Roving everywhere.
Dawn greets me
Sneaking from a park bench
And a rendezvous with cold and sky,
I'm a bum, hungry and lonely;
Milk vanishes from doorsteps at dawn
As I pass.

I'm a prostitute,
Seeking a pick-up from the street.
I have a kid and it cries for bread.
I'm a mother,
Just heard my son died at the Front —
A medal and an empty heart.
I'm a toiler, sweating all day,
But somehow I've more debts to pay.

I'm in the cold,
A youngster, hungry and thin,
My soul cries for love and laughter,
But I'm on this side of the window;
In there, there's fire and laughter
And the warmth of love.

I'm a poet,
And through hunger
And lust for love and laughter
I have turned myself into a voice,
Shouting the pain of the People
And the sunshine that is to be.
                              (1940)

For Laughter

Man's laughter is dead.

I have been peaceful,
Meekly obedient.
Humility spoke from my eyes,
Christ's reflection from my smile;
I craved their love,
They served me hate;
I yearned to be 'brother,'
But was paid with 'bastard.'
Humbly I accepted
'Twas the 'Will of God.'

But I have witnessed
My sisters selling their bodies,
Thousands of them, everywhere . . .
    The factories are slow,
    The bosses want profits,
    My sisters must eat.

I have been awakened
By strange machines
Wiping laughter for ever
From the eyes of my regimented brothers.

I have been shaken,
And tears that I thought long gone
Brimmed my lids
When a starving white said 'Brother!'

I have seen in death
Hate fall away
And black fear and white fear
Twisted into human fear;
And black cries and white cries
Turned into human cries:
And black skins and white skins
Tortured into workers' skins.

I searched for laughter
In the eyes of children,
But soberly they went about
Digging peels from gutters.
Instead of laughter
Death leered at me
From their hungry eyes.

I have learnt to love
Burningly
With the fiercest fire
And I have discarded my humility
And the 'Will of God'
And the stories of my wise teachers.
Arming myself with the wretchedness
In every plain man's life,
And all the to-morrows, my soldiers,
I battle on behalf of that freedom
That will restore the laughter of man!

Freedom's Child

The echoes are dying,
The whisper is gone,
But every tree seems to nod its head,
Is it its ghost . . .?

I
I am China
They call me Le-Yen,
The ricefields own me.
My best years are gone;
I have sweated,
Eaten opium,
And at last I died—
And now I'm going to die again.
But I've heard it, this whisper,
And I love its sound.
I'm China,
But they call me Le-Yen down here.

II
And I am a mother,
Some call me Japan.
I don't want an Empire,
Or a wonderful navy,
I don't care what rate I am—
I have no fight—
All I want
Is my son to return
And food for the children,
A dress for my daughter,
My afternoon tea.
And no uniforms.
I want peace, I want quiet
And my children's love.

That whisper—
What promise does it hold . . . ?

III
My name is Coolie. Untouchable.
I am a jewel,
The brightest in a crown
Of a foreign king.
From my blood
Princes make gold to weight themselves.
I'm an Anna a day, I spit blood when I cough.
I am the floods
And a hundred million starving souls.
I am the droughts
And a hundred million dead.
I am Nehru
I languish in jail.
I am an Anand—
The tears of a tortured soul.
But I've heard this whisper,
My body grows
Bigger!
BIGGER!!
Now there's room for me only here—
No kings or princes.
And I cry:
'Inquilab Zindabad!'
I am India!

IV
I am the gold mines,
Paying huge dividends;
I am the preacher—
Shining car, well fed;
My sermon is race purity,
And God was white and
White men must guard blacks.
I am the banker, Kipling,
And East and West
And the white man's burden.
I am the Institute of Race Relations,
And racial mixture is a crime . . .
I am a half-caste—
Racial mixture is a crime . . .
I am gold,
Fashioned out of beads of sweat of black men;
I am segregation and the pass-law;
I'm eight million slaves . . .
But somewhere, too,

I nurture a volcano,
And out of love
I shall cause a wild eruption
With an aftermath of laughter.

V

Slave of masters, world without choice,
Serving those masters I still bear your voice;
The great lords who rule you are heading for death,
They suck in its vapour with every breath.
Bending your backs to tyranny's yoke,
Taking the full force of every stroke,
The master beasts are marching to death —
I heard it whispered in a dying breath.
The whisper was caught by the Proletarian breeze
And carried away across the seas,
And every sufferer heard the voice,
And in quiet I heard the wind rejoice.
And clear in the twilight the clouds burst wild,
Singing my song — 'Freedom's Child!'

H.I.E. Dhlomo

Because I'm Black

Because I'm black
You think I lack
The talents, feelings and ambitions
That others have;
You do not think I crave positions
That others crave.

Because the people eat and sing
And mate,
You do not see their suffering.
You rate
Them fools
And tools
Of those with power and boastful show;
Not Fate, but fault, has made things so.

Beware! these people, struggling, hold
The last trump card;
Subdue them now you may
'Tis but delay. Another day
When God commands they will be bold . . .
They will strike hard!

The Question
(Beasts or Brothers)

Would you have me as a brother?
Or a revengeful beast?
Would you have us help each other,
Or have our hates increased?

Would you have us stay your progress,
Grip, bruise you like a chain?
Is your aim to halt our progress;
Why? How? What end? What gain?

Would you have us all face upward
And hail the sun and stars?
Or, frustrated, peeved, and both sides forward,
Inflict and nurse Race scars?

Would you have us live despairing?
Starve, kill, revolt and die?
Or free men co-operating:
Wing aiding wing to fly?

Would you have us work together
And live and build in peace?
Or prefer us fight and blather,
And racial hell release?

Would you have us as your neighbours,
Or enemies within?
Are our hopes and patient labours
To end in bloody din?

Brother I am not your neighbour . . .
Was fatal Cain's philosophy:
As thyself so love thy neighbour . . .
Is to be strong, great, wise and free!

from **Valley of a Thousand Hills**

Ah! Purity! Sweet Purity! I thirst!
The Beauty, Glory, I have ever sought!
It shakes and quakes, would slip and melt away
Or laugh at, mock and humble me. Hold still
You gasping craggy heights, you valleys deep!
Sway not you bushy-bearded hills! Dance not
Nor rail at me with happy drunken sounds!
Wild visions crowd and tear and wreck my soul!
My seeing eyes see not! Heavy my ears,
With song appalled! Thoughts claw their way to birth!

Ancestral Spirits great vouchsafe me power
This beauty fierce to seize and rape and make
My own . . . to express! The poet do not jilt.
Give me the words, the depth, the holiness
This magic sight to hold, imprison, sing!
This myriad beauty of the Thousand Land:
The skipping playing ground of tribal gods
Who earth remembering, settled on these hills
And vales, and thought and wrought this thousand-shaped
Earth-heaven: and, Spirits still, to heavenly spheres
Returned, leaving behind them still unchanged
This miracle they breathed for god-like sport.
Here Nkosazana, goddess bright of Light,
Prosperity, Child-birth, and Justice, lived.

'Twas she when tyrant kings with blood reigned harsh,
Rose earthward the afflicted and oppressed
To liberate or soothe and shield from tears,
And justice on the tyrant swift to bring.
And she it was appeared to Mbopha when
From her 'gainst Shaka justice dark he sought.
A Presence fierce in sight there she appeared;
Before the sheen he stood all numb and blind.
When light receded, purged, he understood ! . . .
And struck! because she, not Dingane, spoke.
Nomkhubulwana fair, goddess of love
And song and maiden purity here once
Held sway. For Beauty's gifts were hers to give.

The song and pace now widen out into
A flooded stream all dark and fierce with Wrong!
No longer mine but tortured visions of
The race I see; a groaning symphony
Of grim discordant notes of race and creed,
Of writhing snakes of ideologies
And twanging tunes of clashing colour themes,
Where Wealth and Power and Blood reign worshipped gods,
And Merit, Truth and Beauty serve as slaves!
From mountain tops of Time, Events should rise
Visions resplendent with happy surmise;
But on these heights of Time, Event, I gaze
Into a future tragic with Greed's ways.
With din and pain fraught is the sight!
For hills find we mountains of strife;
For rills deep streams of blood and sweat;
For trees the swelling song of woe;
For herds the broken people of the land;
For heights and depths the depths and heights of woe,
Where joys of life drip hot pain;
Where but to live is sacrifice!

A groaning wail from this Present breaks:
'O native Soul! art dead and ever flown?
Or art thou tame and lost in slavery?
For ages they have tramped, exploited you;
Forever you defy, escape, deceive,
And laugh at them! Forever blooming out
Into new beauties deep and fresh;
Forever chanting songs the Past exudes,
Of swarthy giant men, wise, kingly, proud!
Who midst these beauties of the Thousand Hills,
Forever strove and struck, themselves to wrench
From domination foreign — shameful badge!
Where is the Heart, the Soul, the Purpose of
Our blest ancestral bands? Ah! dig the Past!

Land of the Thousand Valleys if you live,
Still throbs the native Heart, still lives that Soul!
It lingers dumb but whole, unscathed if seared!'
Unsatisfied with tones all calm with hope,
Another in more poignant music thus:
 'This beauty's not my own! My home is not
My home! I am an outcast in my land!
They call me happy while I lie and rot
Beneath a foreign yoke in my dear strand!
Midst these sweet hills and dales, under these stars,
To live and to be free, my fathers fought.
Must I still fight and bear anew the scars?
Must freedom e'er with blood, not sweat, be bought?
You ask me whence these yearning words and wild;
You laugh and chide and think you know me well;
I am your patient slave, your harmless child,
You say . . . so tyrants dreamt as ev'n they fell!
My country's not my own — so will I fight!
My mind is made: I will yet strike for Right.'
With notes all dignified, in sweetness couched,
Still discontent a third now bellowed out
In screech of parlance modern, blunt and sharp:
    'We stood all ravished!
    And spite hope beheld no ray.
    All this is vanished
    For the poet had his say.
    It is the poet's lay
    Will win the day . . .
    The hour of Fate
    Has come! Let's lift our eyes
    To view new skies!
    The Valley of the Hills
    With visions fills!
    At last the native Soul
    Will win the goal.
    There is no power can stand
    This living band!'

In chorus proud and brave the three then joined:
'The Seed of Shaka, Hintsa, Khama and
Moshoeshoe, go, Cetshwayo, and the band
Of Bards of old, cannot forever live
Oppressed. To slavery they will not yield.
Blood boils as they behold both spear and shield:
We'll strike and take! if others will not give!'

Agape burst all the holy graves!
Disturbed Ancestral Spirits rise
And call! A hush falls on the scene!
Obedient smiles the sun! The womb

Of life conceives, and life anew
Begins! Worms wind their way to light!
Wild pulsings throb and course and give
New heart and blood into all tired flesh.
Buds burst into a flower of peace,
And coverts once again mean home;
New flowers midst all the dust are seen —
The flowers which tell the ever-blooming Soul
And Seed of this puissant race and young,
So quick to learn, at growing up so slow . . .
For long the youth of gods! Swift wild life tells
The unbroken roaming Urge in all black veins.
But best of all behold the winging birds
Take to the skies in song! It is our Soul!
It lives! It mocks! It sings! It soars! 'Tis great!
Rich fragrant odours grace the air;
And verdant plants finger their way to the crests!
All earth is purged, and we enthroned!
The picture from the Hills is painted full.
'As it began so never will it end!
And never will it last as now it is!
The Dawn comes soon! The Dawn — and you!'
Whispered the Valley of a Thousand Hills!

Song of the Dawn

Full many a deep disturbance
    These beauteous lands have seen;
When Furies launched their vengeance,
    And smote our peace serene.

At last the stars are gleaming,
    Eternal in their strength!
For storms that seem unceasing,
    To calm must waste at length.

And now the Soul of dawning
    With Light floods all the earth;
Sweet Hopes trips in a-stealing . . .
    This the longed Hour of Birth!
                    (1941)

Not For Me

Not for me the Victory celebrations!
Not for me
Ah! not for me.
I who helped and slaved in the protection
Of their boasted great civilization:
Now sit I in tears 'mid celebrations
Of a war I won to lose,
Of a peace I may not choose.
Before me lies
Grim years of strife,
Who gave my life
To gain—what prize?
In land and sea my brothers buried lie;
The message came, they answered and they fell.
With blood and toil our rights they thought to buy,
And by their loyal stand Race fires to quell.
Now that the War is ended,
Begins my war!
I rise to fight unaided
The wrongs I abhor!
I see the flags of peace in joy unfurled,
And think of my position in the world
They say will come.
And I stand dumb
With wrath! Not victory in the battle field
Those precious things we crave for life will yield.
I see them gathered to decide on peace,
For War, they know, will lead to Man's surcease.
But, Lord, I am not represented;
My presence there is still resented.
Yet where I'm not,
There Christ is not!
For Jesus died and lives for all;
To Him no race is great or small.
And if they meet without the Lord to guide,
They cannot build a Peace that will abide.
The cause of war are Greed, Race, Pride and Power,
Yet these impostors sway peace talks this hour.
How long O Lord before they learn the art
Of peace demands a change in their own heart!
I'll fight! but pray,'Forgive them Father,
Despite their boast and pomp they know not what they do.'
I hate them not; believe I rather
My battle will lead them discover Christ anew.
This is the irony,
This is the agony:
As long as those in power repentance need,
I sit upon the spikes of Wrong and bleed!

Not for me,
Ah! not for me.
The celebrations,
The peace orations.
Not for me,
Yes, not for me
Are victory
And liberty!
Of the Liberty I died to bring in need;
And this betrayal wounds and sears my soul. I bleed.

(1945)

Anonymous

Shantytown

High on the veld upon the plain
And far from streets and lights and cars
And bare of trees, and bare of grass,
Jabavu sleeps beneath the stars.

Jabavu sleeps.
The children cough.
Cold creeps up, the hard night cold,
The earth is tight within its grasp,
The highveld cold without soft rain,
Dry as the sand, rough as a rasp
The frost rimmed night invades the shacks.
Through dusty ground
Through rocky ground
Through freezing ground, the night cold creeps.
In cotton blankets rags and sacks
Beneath the stars Jabavu sleeps.

One day Jabavu will awake
To greet a new and shining day;
The sound of coughing will become
The children's laughter as they play
In parks with flowers where dust now swirls
In strong-walled homes with warmth and light.
Jabavu sleeps. The stars are bright.
                    (1946)

Demetrius Segooa

Praises of the Train
Translated from the Sotho

I am the black centipede, the rusher with a black nose,
drinker of water at the fountain itself of witches,
and whose spells do you say can bewitch me?
I vanquished the sun, man-eater, and the jet-black dark
where the beasts of prey drink blood by day and night —
I, the centipede, great roarer with an inward roar.

My people named me Traveller-to-the-South.
I have altered, not any more a bearer of burdens,
the black calf of the South,
I am the black sorceress,
witch of the day and night;
swift powerful, I have driven on till I hate the road,
I with the fire kindled in my belly.

I have raced and outmatched the horse,
my speed flung the sand in the air
and I won, I the black calf.
At the town where the circumcision drum was beating
I came and said I was from where no one knows,
I come from the unknown, from a far-off country.

They asked me what kind of food I needed
and I answered: none, not like these cowards of yours.
I sleep without food, the all-devourer,
I keep away from the marriage-rites of Ramaesela
for should I enter his enclosure a great cry would rise
like the yell for a leopard among the king's cattle.

At home they say that I am lost —
No pampered child, I am the centipede of the marshes;
hunger does not delay me
nor do I halt from becoming foot-sore,
but the mountains, children of the waste,
demand their price and I pay them.

Not for the sacred spirits do I seek to die,
they who are no man's possession:
but my tribe perish for letting me wander homeless.
I defend the villages from captivity,
brave when the village stands up to danger
and the country says: Where shall I hide them, these cowards?

Ceaselessly on my feet on the iron road
I go falling, falling in the gulleys,
I mimic a river risen in flood
that carries to the mines a man's village.
What can the road owners do to me, the black centipede,
rushing on, fixed to time?

St. J. Page Yako

The Contraction and Enclosure of the Land
Translated from the Xhosa

Thus spake the heirs of the land
Although it is no longer ours.
This land will be folded like a blanket
Till it is like the palm of a hand.
The racing ox will become entangled in the wire,
Too weak to dance free, it will be worn
Out by the dance of the yoke and the plough.
They will crowd us together like tadpoles
In a calabash ladle. Our girls
Will have their lobola paid with paper,
Coins that come and go, come and go.
Blood should not be spilled, so they say
Nowadays, to unite the different peoples;
Until we no longer care for each other,
As a cow licks her calf, when love
And nature urges her to do so.
Can money bring people together?
Yes, a man may have words with his son's wife,
His son need no longer respect her mother.

Yes, we fold up our knees,
It's impossible to stretch out.
Because the land has been hedged in.

Indigenous Work Song

Pass Office Song
Translated into English

Take off your hat.
What is your home name?
Who is your father?
Who is your chief?
Where do you pay your tax?
What river do you drink?
We mourn for our country.

Post-Sharpeville
(1960 – 1976)

Casey Motsisi

The Efficacy of Prayer

They called him Dan the Drunk.
The old people refuse to say how old he was,
Nobody knows where he came from — but they all
Called him Dan the Drunk.
He was a drunk, but perhaps his name was not really Dan.
Who knows, he might have been Sam.
But why bother, he's dead, poor Dan.
Gave him a pauper's funeral, they did.
Just dumped him into a hole to rest in eternal drunkenness.
Somehow the old people are glad that Dan the Drunk is dead.
Ghastly!
They say he was a bad influence on the children.
But the kids are sad that Dan the Drunk is no more.
No more will the kids frolic to the music that used to flow out of his battered
    concertina. Or listen to the tales he used to tell.
All followed him into that pauper's hole.
How the kids used to worship Dan the Drunk!
He was just one of them grown older too soon.
'I'm going to be just like Dan the Drunk,' a little girl said to her parents
    of a night cold while they crowded around a sleepy brazier.
The parents looked at each other and their eyes prayed.
'God Almighty, save our little Sally.'
God heard their prayer.
He saved their Sally.
Prayer. It can work miracles.
Sally grew up to become a nanny . . .
(1960)

Basil Somhlahlo

Who Wants to be Mothered?

Do not do things for me, let me do them.
Think no thoughts for me, let me think them.
You bore me with your thoughts;
Who wants to be mothered?

As a baby, mother carried me,
On her back she bound me tight.
As a boy she let me run.
In front of her she let me run.

As a lad she let me roam,
Away from home I could even roam;
She knew what she was doing
So do not mother me.

On her breast she suckled me, as a baby;
On goat's milk she fed me, as a boy;
But as a lad, I learnt to feed on roots
Far away across the veld.

I knew my home and who my mother was,
She knew I would return and return I did.
Return I did and loving remained.
To trust her I learnt, obey her, never questioned.

Live for me she never tried,
Live for myself, thus did I learn.
I know my goal
So do not mother me.

Show me the way, do not walk the way for me.
My legs are strong, my head not closed, O please not closed.
I know my goal so
Do not mother me.

Enver Docratt

The Slender Child

The slender child is dying in the bush
And the mother beats the broken drum:
Boom! Boom! Spare the heart and take the sheep,
And the pot of grounded meal. Boom! Boom!
The slender child will sin no more.

The Storm

There is a treachery in the bush:
The road has withered in the storm
And mighty men remain
To worship demons and obey.
There is a treachery in the bush:
The sky is washed in pain,
And children talk of sex
Where demons drink the blood and pray.

Dollar Brand (Abdullah Ibrahim)

from **Africa, Music and Show Business**

blues for district six

early one new year's morning
when the emerald bay waved its clear waters against the noisy
    dockyard
a restless south easter skipped over slumbering lion's head
danced up hanover street
tenored a bawdy banjo
strung an ancient cello
bridged a host of guitars
tambourined through a dingy alley
into a scented cobwebbed room
and crackled the sixth sensed district
into a blazing swamp fire of satin sound

early one new year's morning
when the moaning bay mourned in murky waters against the
    deserted dockyard
a bloodthirsty south easter roared over hungry lion's head
and ghosted its way up hanover street
empty
forlorn
and cobwebbed with gloom

where loneliness' still waters meet nostalgia
and morning breaks the city sun and smoke
and towering grey the buildings' murmur
grim subway rumblings in their roots
i scan the vacant faces and sad smiles
and long for home

the night my soul had herringed red
through raucous songs of childhood:
and friends and comic stories long forgotten
were whiskied out of memories dim
to function as narcotic
and silence cruel reality as it screamed
it's neither here nor there

i'm hemisphered
but three
the southern cross and libran scale
and god knows
he knows
where

Mbuyiseni Oswald Mtshali

Boy on a Swing

Slowly he moves
to and fro, to and fro,
then faster and faster
he swishes up and down.

His blue shirt
billows in the breeze
like a tattered kite.

The world whirls by:
east becomes west,
north turns to south;
the four cardinal points
meet in his head.

Mother!
Where did I come from?
When will I wear long trousers?
Why was my father jailed?
                    (1971)

Always a Suspect

I get up in the morning
 and dress up like a gentleman —
A white shirt a tie and a suit.

I walk into the street
to be met by a man
who tells me 'to produce.'

I show him
the document of my existence
to be scrutinized and given the nod.

Then I enter the foyer of a building
to have my way barred by a commissionaire
'What do you want?'

I trudge the city pavements
side by side with 'madam'
who shifts her handbag
from my side to the other,
and looks at me with eyes that say
'Ha! Ha! I know who you are;

beneath those fine clothes
ticks the heart of a thief.'

An Abandoned Bundle

The morning mist
and chimney smoke
of White City Jabavu
flowed thick yellow
as pus oozing
from a gigantic sore.

It smothered our little houses
like fish caught in a net.

Scavenging dogs
draped in red bandanas of blood
fought fiercely
for a squirming bundle.

I threw a brick;
they bared fangs
flicked velvet tongues of scarlet
and scurried away,
leaving a mutilated corpse —
an infant dumped on a rubbish heap —
'Oh! Baby in the Manger
sleep well
on human dung.'

Its mother
had melted into the rays of the rising sun,
her face glittering with innocence
her heart as pure as untrampled dew.

The Detribalised

He was born in Sophiatown,
Or Alexandra, I am not sure,
but certainly not in Soweto.

He skipped school
during playtime
to hock sweets
peanuts, shoelaces,
pilfered in town,
caddied at the golfcourse.

He can write —
only his name;
He can read —
The World:
'Our one and only paper',
The Golden City Post —
murder, rape and robbery.

He has served time
at the 'Fort'.
Prison is no shame,
just as unavoidable
and unpleasant
as going to a dentist.

He's a 'clever'
not a 'moegie';
he never says baas
to no bloody white man.

He wears
the latest Levison's suits
'Made in America';
from Cuthbert's
a pair of Florscheim shoes
'America's finest shoes',
He pays cash
that's why
he's called Mister.

He goes for quality, man,
not quantity, never —
the price is no obstacle.

His furniture is
from Ellis, Bradlow's, exclusive.

Nothing from the O.K. Bazaars
except groceries
and Christmas toys
for their kids
'Very cheap!' says his wife.

Yes, his wife —
also born in the city, Orlando!
she's pretty,
dresses very well:
costumes from Vanité or Millews.
She's very sophisticated,
uses Artra, Hi—Lite

skin lightening cream,
hair straightened,
wears lipstick
a wig, nail polish:
she can dance
the latest 'Monkey'.

He married her
after he had fathered
two kids
to prove her fertility.
There's the occasional
domestic quarrel:
he punches her
a 'blue eye'
to show her
he's the boss.

He takes another cherrie
to the movies
at Lyric or Majestic.
They dine at the Kapitan
and sleep at the Planet.

Maybe they go
to a night session
in a posh shebeen:
jazz, booze
knives and guns.

The wife sees
a 'nyanga'
to bring her man back home.

He runs a car
'60 Impala Chev.
Automatic, sleek.

He knows
he must carry a pass.
He don't care for politics
He don't go to church
He knows Sobukwe
he knows Mandela
They're in Robben Island.
'So what? That's not my business!'

Talismans

Bring me a locust
to fry until its skin turns brown;
the broiled serrated legs exude green marrow,
the tips of a million sunrays stored
in lifeless eyes;
the wings will stay frayed at the edges.

    Give me a stripped rat to skin,
    I'll rip its tiny belly open.
    The trickle of blood will smudge my fingers;
    I'll fashion its fangs into a necklace.
    'A choker of evil spirits!'

Let me have the feathers of an owl,
plucked clean of its vaunted wisdom,
the fluffy down stripped into nakedness,
the indicator of arid yesterday,
the pointer to a bleak tomorrow.

Who will offer me
a few quills of a fat porcupine?
Their sharpness will prick the deadwood,
the hidebound souls of hypocrites;
to prise open the undeciphered scrolls
of vile deeds committed over past centuries.

    The tests are predictable.
    The results will be positive.
              (1980)

Weep not for a Warrior

A warrior drinks the goat's blood for bravery
as a willow in a swamp sucks water
to grow stalwart and stay evergreen.

A warrior never perishes;
he is sustained by the glorious deeds of the departed;
he eats the raw meat of fearlessness
and awaits his canonisation in the realm of heroes,
where all the freedom fighters dwell;
their numerous names are inscribed for posterity
in the massive girth of the baobab tree.

Fear has no roots
strong enough to pierce
the armoured heart of a man in bondage,
whose unbridled anger tears the tiger from its lair,

grabs the lion by its tail,
spears the elephant on its trunk.

Tears were not made
to fall like rain on the grave of the warrior,
to drown the indomitable spirit,
and wash away his halo of martyrdom.

As the clouds of war gather,
and the southern sky frowns with rage,
and the mountains quiver like broth,
and the lightning swords the firmament,
and the clouds melt into cascades of water,
and the gushing torrents collect the corpses
and flush them like logs into a raging sea,
the death knell will echo to every corner.

The warrior will lie there, solemn
in his impregnable casket.
His proud widow and children will say,
  'Weep not for him,
  He was a brave warrior;
  Let him rest on the buffalo-hide bed,
  where his forefathers repose.'

James Matthews

It Is Said

It is said
that poets write of beauty
of form, of flowers and of love
but the words I write
are of pain and of rage

I am no minstrel
who sings songs of joy
mine a lament

I wail of a land
hideous with open graves
waiting for the slaughtered ones

Balladeers strum their lutes and sing tunes of happy times
I cannot join in their merriment
my heart drowned in bitterness
with the agony of what white man's law has done

women of dimbaza and ilinge

women of dimbaza and ilinge
you can now provide for yourself
like the women of sada and limehill
you can toil through the week
with the making of beads
to be sold by well-meaning souls
at three rand fifty to seventy-five
the menfolk, too, have their trade
fine carvers of coffins they are
and the left-over beads
could be used to decorate the dead
of the villages of sorrow

Mike Dues

Armies of the Night

I went and lay
an empty shell
way by the side
of the road to oblivion
now I am bare
she has to bear
knowledge other than shadow
to satisfy
the majestic boot
that prefers the carded self
she will bear
and grin
for happiness to her
is but a rubber stamp

Hunger Wrote the Epitaph

this city
pregnant with hunger
grinding underfoot
tons of cemented sweat
whose swimming pools
are catchment areas of tears
whose towered names
refuse to listen
where cities
are different nightfalls
and one neon lit
the other lit
for stilling the hunger of men coming home
ask him
who only plods mechanical feet
the marvels of the day
ask him
who stares at you from sockets
gouged by his day
ask him
who knows his place
by the ages of the day
and could not befriend the moon here:
I know you remember
'our father ....'

Mandlenkosi Langa

The Pension Jiveass

I lead her in,
A sepia figure 100 years old.
Blue ice chips gaze
And a red slash gapes:
'What does she want?'
I translate: 'Pension, sir.'
'Useless kaffir crone,
Lazy as the black devil.
She'll get fuck-all.'
I translate.
'My man toiled
And rendered himself impotent
With hard labour.
He paid tax like you.
I am old enough to get pension.
I was born before the great wars
And saw my father slit your likes' throats!'
I don't translate, but
She loses her pension anyhow.

Bicca Maseko

King Mzilikazi Revisited

In the beginning
I was a ghost in your night
An assegai flash in a Mosega night
Later
I was a ballet dancer
In your dreams
Dancing, laughing and laughed at
A cabaret artist in your night clubs
Singing and clowning
I am
Once again
A Limpopo nightmare
A stray bullet . . . . .

Mafika Mbuli

The Miners

This dungeon
Makes the mind weary
Kneaded with the sight of
A million stones
Passing through my hands
I see the flesh sticking like hair
On thorns
Against the grating rocks
Of these hills dug for gold,
And life is bitter here.
Crawling through the day
In a sleepwalker's dream,
Frightening the night away with my snores,
I dream of the diminished breath
Of miners planted in the stones —
The world is not at ease
But quakes under the march of our boots
Tramping the dust under our feet . . .
Click, clack, our picks knock for life
Until the eyes are dazed
Counting the rubble of scattered stones.

Day and night are one.
But I know each day dawns
And the heated sun licks every shrub dry
While we who burrow the earth
Tame the dust with our lungs.

Click, clack, we knock with picks
And our minds
Drone with the voices of women
Harassing our loins
To force courage into the heart.
Wherefore might we scorn their sacrifice
Made in blood,
Greater that the blood of men
Sacrificed to the earth
For its possession!
And so
Clap, scrape
With our hands manacled
With weariness
We mine
All our lives
Till the mind is numb
And ceases to ask . . .

Nkathazo ka Mnyayiza

Bad Friday
1972

Crammed breast-to-back;
they gabbed,
              shouted defiantly:
gulped intoxicating drinks
with the Zionist's drum beat
chanting the joyous song
of the gritting wheels underneath;
bounding home or to congregations
in tobacco musty township train
when suddenly,
              laughter stopped
death approached
              and the dust filled the air
as they hit the drought-seared earth;
wheels spun in air,
    bodies sprawled
              dead on living
    while blood flowed
from the dead and injured,
along the ripped-up line;
while a cock peeped
from a Glen Tea packet
              to breathe fresh air;
he crowed,
              and ducked back in.

Forgotten People

Broken
rusty
and hanging gates
fallen leaves on unswept yards
where mangy dogs stretch out their empty beings
and where fowls peck fruitlessly at unwashed dishes
I saw him the old man on an old bench seated
leaning his old back against the crumbling mud walls
thoughts far off man's reach and sight
and like the setting sun
he gave way to the dying embers of life
and slowly he slouched into bed
with a dry and an empty stomach
to await another empty day or death.

84

Kneel and Pray

I have seen many white stars,
but haven't seen any black;
            but i know that
one day

            from the north
the long black star will come;
black clouds then will scud around it,

        then

            when it shakes

you'll shiver like reeds,

        then
                when it screams

you'll kneel and pray.

Zulu Molefe

Black Zionist Meeting

All the unsung poets
of this religion
all those who swear undying
loyalty with jehovah
are present tonight

'What will we say
on the cross?'
thunders the bearded preacher
as he leads his flock
like Moses out
   of the house of bondage
to meet jehovah
in prayer and song

For a few hours
    they
       are
          free.

To Paint a Black Woman

clothe her in a black doek
    black pinafore
and a faded blouse
(forget her feet
she can be without shoes
for all we care!)

add
 her look of resignation
with those sad eyes
which seem to be asking
that unspoken question —
'where have you been?'
or
'what have i done now?'

Stanley Mogoba

Cement

An unprecedented abundance of cement
Below, above and all round
A notorious capacity to retain cold
Without an equal facility for warmth

Inside is captured a column of air
And a solid mass of human substance
A pertinent question poses itself:
Which loses heat to which?

As complete an enclosure as possible
Throwing its presence all around
Until recognised by all five senses
Achieving the results of refrigeration

Hovering relentlessly is the stubborn stillness
Permeating both solid and gas
A free play of winged imagination
And the inevitable introspection
Stretch themselves painfully over
The reluctant minutes of the marathon day.

Stanley Motjuwadi

White Lies

Humming Maggie.
Hit by a virus,
the Caucasian Craze,
sees horror in the mirror.
Frantic and dutifully
she corrodes a sooty face,
braves a hot iron comb
on a shrubby scalp.
I look on.

I know pure white,
a white heart,
white, peace, ultimate virtue.
Angels are white
angels are good.
Me I'm black,
black as sin stuffed in a snuff-tin.
Lord, I've been brainwhitewashed.

But for Heaven's sake God,
just let me be.
Under cover of my darkness
let me crusade.
On a canvas stretching from here
to Dallas, Memphis, Belsen, Golgotha,
I'll daub a white devil.
Let me teach black truth.
That dark clouds aren't a sign of doom,
but hope. Rain. Life.
Let me unleash a volty bolt of black,
so all around may know black right.

Njabulo S. Ndebele

The Man of Smoke

Strapped to my aunt's back
I find warmth
We walk through many streets
I don't know which,
but I know when we turn.
Even in my blanket,
I can feel the dust of the wind
pecking at me, like many needles,
but I cling to my aunt,
her back is warm and moist.

There are voices in this house
I don't know which,
I'm in the warm darkness
of my blanket.
'Mzalwane' Voices greet.
'Bazalwane' auntie answers.
Then I am unstrapped
to the gaze of silence
to the gloom of a candle
to the frightening stares
of a huge face of a person of wood
with teeth as big as fingers
smoke comes out of his mouth,
smoke comes out of his wicked smile.

Put me back, auntie, put me back,
it is cold here
but my words are not lips
they are my hands
clutching at her dress.

She puts me under a table,
but I move out to a corner.
A drum begins the beat:
GOGOM GOM . . . . . GOGOM GOM . . . . .
and there is song and dance
wild song and dance
and I am watching alone
from a corner; my corner.
I am wide eyed
I am shorter than the table
and dancing legs are massive pillars.
I cling to my corner
lest I am crushed by dance.

I cling to my corner
watching my aunt do funny things;
she is mad, quite mad:
all are mad here,
and smoke issues out of
the ugly person's mouth,
smoke is filling the room,
the room is grey smoke now,
GOGOM GOM .....GOGOM GOM .....
Alleluya! Alleluya ....
round round round they dance
round the table
GOGOM GOM ..... GOGOM GOM .....
Alleluya! Alleluya .....

I am a child watching
from a corner
I am a child clinging
to my corner

I am a child fearing
to be crushed.
I watch my aunt who is mad
quite mad.
All are mad here.
They kneel before the face of smoke
they cry, they shriek,
they breathe in gasps
they say a wind must enter them
they are mad quite mad,
rising to sing and dance and clap hands.
I fear.
I fear people with the wind, praying
like a cow bellowing.

Strapped to my aunt's back,
I find warmth
we walk through many streets
I don't know which,
but I know we are going home now.
I know that we are passing other people
singing, drumming and hand-clapping
down the street:
'These are the wicked dogs
who broke away from our sect
'Curse them, God. May they burn.'
Even in the noise of the wind
I can hear auntie's spittle
cursing the dogs on the tarred road.

But I am warm in the blanket,
it is dark and warm and moist inside,
and I dream of the man of wood
standing next to my bed in the dark,
choking me with his smoke,
and I cry.
'Poor boy, you are hungry,' auntie says.

I Hid My Love

I hid my love in the sewerage
Of a city; and when it was decayed,
I returned:
I returned to the old lands,
The old lands
Where old men and old women
Laugh all day
Until their lungs are as dry as dust:
Where old men and old women
Talk all day
About the weather, about proverbs, about fields . . .
About trivial things:
Where they talk all day
About trivial things . . .

There was I in the wilderness,
Outlandish years dull
Like the rings of a rusted bell.
I stood aloof when the cows
Spread their moo across the rural greens,
I was king,
I was king of the bees,
I ruled over the honey,
I ruled over the milk pail
Full of white bubbles.
Ha! Ha! I held my hollow belly
In laughter when a hen dropped an egg.
My arms akimbo,
I knew the secrets of the world,
I knew the secret pleasures
The better pleasures,
And God, let me lie on the grass
At the entrance of life - unwanted life.
Below the bottom of life,
My love lay drowned in the stench,
Of course I knew it
I knew my love was dead;
But oh no, let me lie unbothered
On the grass at the entrance of life,

Let me break the bonds that make me me.
Let me drift in the wilderness of callousness,
Let me drift an unidentified soul . . .

And when the fumes of decayed love
Were unfurled unto the winds,
and they covered the plains and the greens,
And their rot chewed by the trees,
And their rot sung
By choirs of drunken birds,
I knew I had lost,
God, I knew I had lost;
O who am I? Who am I?
I am the hoof that once
Grazed in silence upon the grass,
But now rings like a bell on tarred streets.

from   **Five Letters to M.M.M.**

Like the shrill of a violin,
Like a wind against a blade of grass,
The purls of blood through the veins;
                into the heart,
The white dream of your brown face, my love,
Motions into a calm ecstasy
The black veins of the dying
Leaves of the tree that is my heart;
And a wind of faces — your faces —
Blows always and softly
Against the hut of my memories
Like a soft motion of the clouds
In the night of your eyes.

By the passing day
The leaves grow greener;
By the passing day
I blush with reverence
At the white silence
Of your dignity,
And by the passing day, my love,
Fearing . . .
Fearing, my plum,
Fearing to uncleave the tongues of my heart,
A pride in your self,
A pride in your laughter,
In which the gaieties of my hopes
Are gathered like milk-drops in a breast;
A pride in a vision of your wedding day,
And the softness of its night,

Armed with the power of legitimacy,
Makes me one with you
In an unspoken love that binds
The soils, that binds the winds;
That binds the soil and the wind
With the flesh and the music of the dead.

Now, on a bed of grass,
I shall lie,
And in your absence
Listen to the nearness of you,
In the sound of the leaves, the grass,
The dust rising in the wind, the bird,
And in the calm flow of my blood,
Till I am whole in my self
                in yourself,
And in the wholeness of myself,
                in yourself.

Motshile wa Nthodi

Standard Fifty-Eight

Born on Saturday,
nineteen forty-eight.
After eight years,
my mother bought me a
    cheap slate for eight pence
    and took me to school.

Monday to Friday
in black and white,
from eight to two o'clock,
we planted tomatoes
and played football.

At the age of eighteen,
I passed standard eight
and became Baas Groen's
    good garden boy.

Today I'm twenty-eight
    years old,
    reading form fourteen,
    working in a garage,
    easy job —
            petrol attendant
for eight rands per month,
    easy job.

I wish I could pass standard
    fifty-eight,
            in cooking
    and become Mrs Beach's
    careless kitchen boy,
for eight cents per week.

Oh!
What an easy job.

South African Dialogue

Morning Baas,
Baas,
Baas Kleinbaas says,
I must come and tell
Baas that,
Baas Ben's Baasboy says,
Baas Ben want to see
Baas Kleinbaas if
Baas don't use
Baas Kleinbaas,
Baas.

Tell
Baas Kleinbaas that,
Baas says,
Baas Kleinbaas must tell
Baas Ben's Baasboy that,
Baas Ben's Baasboy must tell
Baas Ben that,
Baas says,
If Baas Ben want to see
Baas Kleinbaas,
Baas Ben must come and see
Baas Kleinbaas here.

Thank you
Baas.
I'll tell
Baas Kleinbaas that,
Baas says,
Baas Kleinbaas must tell
Baas Ben's Baasboy that,
Baas Ben's Baasboy must tell
Baas Ben that,
Baas says,
If Baas Ben want to see
Baas Kleinbaas,
Baas Ben must come and see
Baas Kleinbaas here,
Baas
Goodbye Baas.

Baas Kleinbaas,
Baas says,
I must come and tell
Baas Kleinbaas that,
Baas Kleinbaas must tell
Baas Ben's Baasboy that,
Baas Ben's Baasboy must tell

Baas Ben that,
Baas says,
If Baas Ben want to see
Baas Kleinbaas,
Baas Ben must come and see
Baas Kleinbaas here,
Baas Kleinbaas.

Baasboy,
Tell Baas Ben that,
Baas Kleinbaas says,
Baas says,
If Baas Ben want to see me
(Kleinbaas),
Baas Ben must come and
See me (Kleinbaas) here.

Thank you
Baas Kleinbaas,
I'll tell
Baas Ben that,
Baas Kleinbaas says,
Baas says,
If Baas Ben want to see
Baas Kleinbaas,
Baas Ben must come and see
Baas Kleinbaas here,
Baas Kleinbaas.
Goodbye
Baas Kleinbaas.

Baas Ben,
Baas Kleinbaas says,
I must come and tell
Baas Ben that,
Baas says,
If Baas Ben want to see
Baas Kleinbaas,
Baas Ben must come and see
Baas Kleinbaas there,
Baas Ben.
Baas Ben,
Baas Be-ne . . . .
Baas Ben.
Goodbye
Baas Ben.

Jennifer Davids

Searching for Words

Searching for words
to contain the morning
I looked beyond the line of trees
at the white sky
hung in the branches

And words swarmed out
like bits of black grit
from the dark spreading pine
cutting the sky
and darkening my mind
till I turned away

turned back to a garden
overgrown with words
sharp as blades

I searched
till bleeding
I found
a flower
with a face
black as the sun

Location Fires

Beneath my eyelids
the landscape is heavy
the people are buried in ground-
clinging shapes of houses

From Langa to Nyanga
the fires are hidden
the landscape is flattened
frightened and silenced

Where are the fires
for me to believe in
where are the tongues of flame
to lick and conquer the dark

In answer the black body
of the sky rears up

loud with roaring
voices of the stars

The stars tonight
are blue backyard fires
studding the black
location of the sky

Poem for my Mother

That isn't everything, you said
on the afternoon I brought a poem
to you hunched over the washtub
with your hands
the shrivelled
burnt granadilla
skin of your hands
covered by foam.

And my words
slid like a ball
of hard blue soap
into the tub
to be grabbed and used by you
to rub the clothes.

A poem isn't all
there is to life, you said
with your blue-ringed gaze
scanning the page
once looking over my shoulder
and back at the immediate
dirty water

and my words
being clenched
smaller and
smaller.

Jiggs

Doornfontein

Doornfontein
ek sê
is not like it was

Rollicking full of life
you met all the manne
everywhere.

Those ous from Corrie
or the Ville musn't
come make shit here
we Dorrie owens
won't take their cac.

Throbbing and bursting
shebeens and brothels,
Ou Cecil Rhodes and
Barney Barnato must
shit
in their graves
to check what
is happening in their
old koeksters.

Nay there's no shit here,
the lanies we get on with
they are just like us.

And now they are
bulldozing the place down
there's hardly anyone left;
except the whores and oere
and of course all
the Mac Fuggers
looking for meat.

Sometime we going to
Bulldoze down their
Homes ek sê
And send them to a
Township and see
How they like it.

Hey man, all the
High Bucks come
From Doorie.

What High Bucks ek sê?

No Umfo, Doorie
Was the place
There were play-whites
And there still are,
But just like Sophiatown,
And Jeppe and so on . . .
They moving us all out
Of town
Making scars on our
Lives and in Josie
But Doorie will
Always be Doorie
Ek sê.

C.D. Noble

Who is the Rain?

Dedication: To Dan

Didn't it rain? Well, didn't it?
The night of the 18th,
Didn't it hail
Saturday?
Yeah! it stormed January
Yep! in Jeppestown
Coming twa, twa, twang
bullets slumping walls
down in that sloot where
my mother used to play
barefooted when she was growing up in Main Street
and
ricochetted
        weight and crush of hailstones
        damned
        Concrete'll have to swim
        Granite to float
        Iron and steel to tread
        water
   warily

We're welling up
        we're water and ice
freezing fire the heat could not thaw
             we're the poor
clashing with modern motors
crashing plate-glassed pioneers obscure
behind a uniform, armed,
standing guard
against the frosted dark

Look!
   with pangas and choppers
   how the children play
   in townships now
   targets for guns
   tasting slaughter for blood
from our rain-goddesses
testing patient suffering
who best can bear
the acts of God
levelling off
massed clouds barricaded
we lean on this collapsed

city shrinking our black urban culture
cleaned up
for pumped-up consumption at the Brooke
where earning bread Ipi-Tombi
actresses and actors
play

What play is this?
   we can't go, outcast, barred
                black
                the skies
                the dams are bursting

We're drops of life
the tense surface
drowning death
built new in
reeking vile
septic houses and plagued pipes
floating sewage
retching the offal of
long years we've fed on
disease we're used to

We're living waters, immune,
springing from sources, like history, like heaven,
that cannot be banned,
exiled,
or courted:

'When it rains, it rains'
   and fine ladies'll take off more than shoes
in the tidal forceful time
                rouge, powder and
                lipstick
                mascara too
the complete cosmetic
facade
before
graced in new identities
we'll smile
one week-working day, brightly
and greet, convention-like, discovered
Brothers and Sisters saying
'Well, didn't it rain, didn't it?'

Mongane Wally Serote

Alexandra

Were it possible to say,
Mother, I have seen more beautiful mothers,
A most loving mother,
And tell her there I will go,
Alexandra, I would have long gone from you.

But we have only one mother, none can replace,
Just as we have no choice to be born,
We can't choose mothers;
We fall out of them like we fall out of life to death.

And Alexandra,
My beginning was knotted to you,
Just like you knot my destiny.
You throb in my inside silences
You are silent in my heart-beat that's loud to me.
Alexandra often I've cried.
When I was thirsty my tongue tasted dust,
Dust burdening your nipples.
I cry Alexandra when I am thirsty.
Your breasts ooze the dirty waters of your dongas,
Waters diluted with the blood of my brothers, your children,
Who once chose dongas for death-beds.
Do you love me Alexandra, or what are you doing to me?

You frighten me, Mama,
You wear expressions like you would be nasty to me,
You frighten me, Mama,
When I lie on your breast to rest, something tells me,
You are bloody cruel.
Alexandra, hell
What have you done to me?
I have seen people but I feel like I'm not one,
Alexandra what are you doing to me?
I feel I have sunk to such meekness!
I lie flat while others walk on me to far places.
I have gone from you, many times,
I come back.
Alexandra, I love you;
I know
When all these worlds became funny to me,
I silently waded back to you
And amid the rubble I lay,
Simple and black.
                    (1972)

City Johannesburg

This way I salute you:
My hand pulses to my back trousers pocket
Or into my inner jacket pocket
For my pass, my life
Jo'burg City.
My hand like a starved snake rears my pockets
For my thin, ever lean wallet,
While my stomach groans a friendly smile to hunger,
Jo'burg City.
My hand like a starved snake tears my pockets
Don't you know?
Jo'burg City, I salute you;
When I run out or roar in a bus to you,
I leave behind me, my love,
My comic houses and people, my dongas and my ever
    whirling dust,
My death,
That's so related to me as a wink to the eye.
Jo'burg City
I travel on your black and white roboted roads,
Through your thick iron breath that you inhale
At six in the morning and exhale from five noon.
Jo'burg City
That is the time when I come to you,
When your neon flowers flaunt from your electrical wind,
That is the time when I leave you,
When your neon flowers flaunt their way through the falling
    darkness
On your cement trees.
And as I go back, to my love,
My dongas, my dust, my people, my death,
Where death lurks in the dark like a blade in the flesh,
I can feel your roots, anchoring your might, my feebleness
In my flesh, in my mind, in my blood,
And everything about you says it,
That, that is all you need of me.
Jo'burg City, Johannesburg,
Listen when I tell you,
There is no fun, nothing, in it,
When you leave the women and men with such frozen
    expressions,
Expressions that have tears like furrows of soil erosion,
Jo'burg City, you are dry like death,
Jo'burg City, Johannesburg, Jo'burg City.

A Poem

Kneel down woman, naked as you are,
Let your heavy head hang down,
And the milk of your breast
And the weight of your back,
Pull you down;
Take a look at the thighs
And see.
The world that God wrote with his big fingers
Were they hesitant fingers?
They wrote a story that we live but do not understand.
Kneel down, woman,
We the born shall lie and hide on your back,
While you take a look.
The truth is that you are seeing an arrangement,
There's water, is it salty? There's blood,
That is salty.
Kneel down, woman, naked as you are.
We are waiting, we want to know.

(Saluting Mother and Child sculpture by Dumile)

What's in this Black 'Shit'

It is not the steaming little rot
In the toilet bucket,
It is the upheaval of the bowels
Bleeding and coming out through the mouth
And swallowed back,
Rolling in the mouth,
Feeling its taste and wondering what's next like it.

Now I'm talking about this;
'Shit' you hear an old woman say,
Right there, squeezed in her little match-box
With her fatness and gigantic life experience,
Which makes her a child,
'Cause the next day she's right there,
Right there serving tea to the woman
Who's lying in bed at 10 a.m. sick with wealth,
Which she's prepared to give her life for
'Rather than you marry my son or daughter.'

This 'Shit' can take the form of action;
My younger sister under the full weight of my father,
And her face colliding with his steel hand,
' 'Cause she spilled sugar that I work so hard for'
He says, not feeling satisfied with the damage his hands
Do to my yelling little sister.

I'm learning to pronounce this 'Shit' well,
Since the other day,
At the pass office,
When I went to get employment,
The officer there endorsed me to Middelburg,
So I said, hard and with all my might, 'Shit!'
I felt a little better;
But what's good, is, I said it in his face,
A thing my father wouldn't dare do.
That's what's in this black 'Shit'.

A Poem on Black and White

if i pour petrol on a white child's face
and give flames the taste of his flesh
it won't be a new thing
i wonder how i will feel when his eyes pop
and when my nostrils sip the smell of his flesh
and his scream touches my heart
i wonder if i will be able to sleep;
i understand alas i do understand
the rage of a whiteman pouring petrol on a black child's face
setting it alight and shooting him in a pretoria street,
pretoria has never been my home
i have crawled its streets with pain
i have ripped my scrotal sack at every door i intended entering
     in that city
and jo'burg city has never seen me, has never heard me
the pain of my heart has been the issue of my heart
sung by me
freezing in the air
but who has not been witness to my smile?
yet, alexandra's night shadow is soaked and drips with my tears.

Death Survey

i had a dream
true like i'm black like this
conflict.
a dream fell on my head that sleeps still like a stone
my head on the bed
the stone in the donga
i had a dream last night
it fell like a feather into my sleep.
a friend came running into the yard and his face was like a horror
a death running wildly loose
when some guys i know came running after him
charging

like dogs so vicious
barking and chasing a cow from a dustbin
my friend came rushing into my house
I ran
could not keep my eyes off from the sparkling knives
dangling over my shoulders
and bricks flying over my head like this
we ran
i was calling my friend's name
he called mine too
and we could not keep off from that gaping donga
which was swallowing my scream and desperately needed my life
why did gatsha come
because there he was holding some meeting with the old leg of the past
sitting in a circle.
i saw them take a kerrie and try to beat out some brain
out of a boy who was kneeling and trying to scream
frightened
i ran loose
to frank's place at ninth avenue and found that the bulldozer
    had been there
before me
i stumbled over bricks
they bit my toes like hungry rats
and something was in my ear
a cockroach
desperately wanting to hide inside my ear
its long legs frantic
its sharp small head digging right through
cruel
even screams don't come in a dream like this
why
this bloody bulldozer had done a good job and its teeth
    dripped blood;
bricks-pillars-hunks-of-concrete-zincs--broken-steps-doors-
    broken-glasses-crooked window-panes broken-flower-
                                pots-planks-twisted-shoes
lay all over the show
like a complete story,
i ran
my toes bleeding
and i held my heart in my right hand
like a jacket.

Introit

I have lain on my back
flat like a long dead reptile
I lie here while my load clutches my heart like a frightened child
And the horrors of my stomach throb to my eyes
I am a black manchild
I am he who has defeated defeat
I am a surprise which surprises me
The load of the day leaves my shoulders red and bruised
But alas
the Chest of the night heaves into my eyes
The whore's scream and the barking dogs are my companions
The snap of life and the making of death have woven my strides
My thick footsteps pulsate on black shadows
They rumble, rumble like a journey with a destination
Aaahw the blackmanchild

I have lain on my back dead just like pulled out weeds
while blood flowed in me like a river
My pores have been holes pouring out sweat which flooded lies
I have built the day like every man has
I have broken the day to shadows which came and lay gently over my house
I am no big blackman
I am a blackmanchild

I have tamed the stallion-woman beneath me
I have held children's hands in mine and led them
Alas the children
They have looked up at me as if my eyes were ripe fruit dangling from a tree
the children have seen the sun shine into my eyes
they have seen my face glow silver with the light of the moon
maybe they have heard me weep too
for I have wept
Lord I wept
my heart bleeds through my eyes
for indeed my eyes are a bloody memory

from No Baby Must Weep

let me hold your hand
black mother let me hold your hand and walk with you
let me feel the odour of your sweat as it falls from your
body and mirages into the air
let the warmth and sweat of your hand
soak into mine
your hands
these hands which have been wrecked by their toil
they have held me in that moment when i laboured to

108

to open my eye
may i hold your hand now
my eye is open and my chin has hair
i come back to you, to hold your hand and let's walk in the street
that is where i have been where you never wanted me to be
let me hold your hand and walk with you
in my kingdom
this is my kingdom which is ruled by the whistle that tears
into the dark
like a sharp blade through a piece of cloth
here i used to criss-cross the street from yard to yard
below the fences which now and then teethed my trousers
or shirt as if to admonish me
that is what i thought
because as i crept beneath the fences and darkness
i could feel your huge eye glittering, twinkling through my
street secrets
in moments when i pinned a little girl into a wrecked automobile
and i groped her body and found out how i came to this world
mama
she was a little sweet thing with eyes spilling fear
and her lips clayed words which froze in my head
words which i never knew their meaning
they used to fall on my bosom and when i slept i heard them
and the flame in my little loin leapt to my heart
in memory of my kingdom
this my mother
that shop veranda that you now see
with bricks long baked in the sun and in the wind and in the rain
looking as if any minute pus might spill out of them,
that shop there
with pillars no longer standing high and fat like a merchant
but crooked and weary like an old ill woman
and the miriam makeba pepsi cola advert saying drink pepsi cola
that closed door, those now sealed windows
looking like gagged mouths and blindfolded eyes
there is my one-time kingdom
we used to summon our truths with whistles
we used to get a clue of what you said or never said while
we sat there
talking
laughing
crying
and i don't know how many times some parts of your body were called
named
talked about
mocked
and always when i walked alone and saw some mothers, fathers
it was as if they were walking there naked
sometimes i laughed alone
sometimes i felt ashamed

when their suits or overalls were just transparent
and i saw them and my kingdom's voices described them
you know
eddy said vusi's mother's breasts were so long, so long she
had to tie them around her body six times every morning
and they say they caught ma-Dlamini fidgeting with her late
husband's fly zip
that is why her fat-koeks are so tasty
it was nice at that veranda
but at times i could not sleep after some sessions
that is when your huge eye now and then stared at me
and i did not know what to do
i loved my kingdom
in my kingdom
sometimes my soft palms felt the juice of the fruits
which at times soiled my hands
sometimes muscled them into a man's
and you sometimes said things and i knew you were lying
you know what they said at school, they said we must bandage
our wounds
and that day when i missed the ball and kicked a stone and
blood and pain held my toe
tlogi said i must pour soil on that mess
and it healed
why did they say it is a sin to sleep with a woman before you marry
because i saw nothing wrong when Bra-Moss did with sis-dinah and
sis-maureen
they all liked it
and tlogi said Bra-Moss was a real man
and i thought so but the priest and the church and the benches
and the incense and the smell of the perfume of women in church
frightened me
like a finger pointing at me
but tlogi said he would never go to church
and you hated tlogi but i loved him
he used to make me laugh that is all and he taught me so many
things like
if he did not get a girl
tlogi went up to the veld
pumped and pumped and pulled and when i did it it was nice
why did you not like tlogi
i wonder where tlogi is now

mama
you know you never let me become a caddie
or a garden-boy
let's stop here a little mama
do you still think i must go to church
and then
do you still want me to go to school

110

and then
i do not know because i don't want to go to church and i don't
want to go to school
are you disappointed
i am disappointed because i did not become a caddie or a
garden-boy
because then the boys used to laugh at me and i really felt
okay
hold my hand let's go
do you love my father
he looks funny doesn't he
with spectacles tight with wire and a torn overall reading a
newspaper trying to catch some horses and complaining about
the prime minister and the laws and the nat party
fearing the police and dead scared of white people
do you love my father
ja
i love him too
i don't know why though

i am your son my mother i am my father's son
cup your hands beneath my breast
let the waters of my wounds flow and wash these
hands that made me
these hands clayed me in that moment
when the river flowed when the river ebbed
when the river burst
and the flesh broke
and the water became flesh when the flames burnt agony
ecstasy
god turning away leaving his shadows prolonged in some
wretched room
i emerge a wound in my gut
using broken tongues and a bleeding heart
kneeling on worn-out knees
never in terms with peace
frantic
like a lady's frock blown by wild wind
i emerge
to tide on my throbbing wound and flow into its rhythm
this wound

this man, this, my brother
if you can eat while my eyes fall into pits with hunger
if you can laugh while my eyes are big darts of tears,
don't call yourself my brother,
you are a man passing by the road, destined to be the
issue of my memories

111

i am the man you will never defeat
i will be the one to plague you
your children are cursed
if you walk this earth, where i too walk
and you tear my clothes and reach for my flesh
and tear my flesh to reach my blood
and you spill my blood to reach my bones
and you smash my bones and hope for my soul
the wind and the mountains and the stars
the sun the moon
saw you
i am the man you will never defeat
my song will merge with the breeze
my tears will freeze in time
you will walk the earth whose dust is my bones
and the sun will set like my eyes when they close for
the last time
and the moon will shine on my scream
i
i am the man you will never defeat
when the trees rattle you shall hear my last footsteps
this won't be your world
i am the man you will never defeat
i will be your shadow, to be with you always
and one day
when the sun rises
the shadows will move, heaving like a tired chest
there shall be millions of shadows
heaving
and the earth shall be cold
and the river will freeze
and the plants will refuse to grow
and the earth shall be dark
and the river shall be dark
and we will be alone
no man can defeat another man
we can sing together
make each other together
we can eat together
make the world together
no man can defeat another man
i turn to you mother whose warmth i felt with my
unripe flesh
hold my hand, your son is a man

let me seep into africa
let this water
this sea
seep into me own me
and break my face into its moods
break my chest

112

break my heart into its fathoms where no hands reach
let the salt of this sea
settle down like a dove come home, into the wounds that
this earth made in my bosom
ah
let this water, this sea
these waves
these colours
this movement
this wide deep blue solid reality break me down like it has rocks
africa
where humilty seeps into rocks and roots
singing the heart-breaking tune
africa
harness your cow . . .

i can say
i
i have gone beyond the flood now
i left the word on the flood
it echoes
in the depth the width
i am beyond the flood

i can say
these eyes
this water this river this flood
washed me
i can say
one day the word will break
i can say
one day the laughter will break
i can say
one day the sky will weep
i can say one day
this flower
will stand in the bright bright sun
this flower will have no petals
one day
ah
africa
is this not your child come home
                    (1975)

113

Child of the Song

(for james matthews)

I
so you heard the night break into a laughter
when the dogs began to howl
and now you pass the day
having heard the scream of cats making love beneath broken automobiles
and your memory
like your eyes
like your whiskers
was witness to it all
otherwise why would you ask me about nina simone
your eyes say nothing nice about the minutes you carried
nor your whiskers
because they smell of alcohol
and your memory keeps throbbing behind your eyes
otherwise why would you sing with ausi miriam
about the empty days
and the nights which shattered your sleep
child of the song
tell us

II
remember
how we used to sit in the womb of the dawn
crushing the days that the future held
popping them
as if they were bugs troubling our night
remember
and we staggered into the mourning into the street
where everything screamed: sonofabitch!

III
yes, the day was not ours nor the night
remember how someone's baby rushed out of the tenth floor
and crushed on the tar
his blood splashing on the flower petals in the garden
so you heard the laughter of the law
what will you say to your son
mourn?
or my son, every mourning is a dangerous alley
yes
prophets claim the future
and the present destroys them

so
child of the song, sing don't cry
with song and dance we defied death
remember
like

the heavens are blue because they are empty
and
beware, my brother, of park benches
sitting there
is the last thing a fighter must do
                              (1978)

Time Has Run Out

The bright eye of the night keeps whispering
when it paves and pages the clouds
it is knowledgeable about hideous nights
when it winks and keeps winking like that
it is like a breathing burning wood —
i feel looked at
walking and silent like this in the night
in this strange land which mutes screams.
the night
with its vague and bright eye-ball
which bears boot-prints and flags
eats away into the bone of the distance of my life
this i know,
and the night knows it too
so
the bright eye of the night keeps whispering and whispering
and the stars with their distance
keep whistling and whistling
throbbing on my memory about the distances we made

yes —
we did make distances
whose milestones are, as we all know
 broken droplets of blood which are now splashed
and are scattered on the streets
on fences
and on walls of houses we live in
and on ceilings
on floors and on desks
even on floors of land-rovers.
i said i feel looked at
walking this silent night like this
alone —
cars, with their treacherous big eyes
stare —
and speed past me, leaving their red glow with me
leaving me with the night
whose thick darkness touches my eye-balls
and keeps dancing into my face
with every footstep i make;
i walk the night of this land

115

i hear crickets chirp
and see prostitutes at street corners
feel shirt and underpants stick to my flesh
and i count the red lights along the village road
smell the green of the tall grass
i'm all over this little town
and,
the stars keep whistling and whistling.
listen —
these fucking stars
whistled like this once long ago
when one man
walked like all of us do
and then he was naked
and then he was chained on the leg
and then he was on the floor covered with a blanket
in a land rover
destined to make 1 000 km in that state
to another cell

where he woke up one morning
naked
chained
alone
with brain damage, his blanket wet
his eyes strange as they said;
and i dare say
his damaged memory told him now, that he was
in his cell
chained on the leg
wet and naked
alone
the 45th to have made it
into the hands of mad men who believe in God
yet these men did not know
that this man knew
he would make it for his funeral
that the people would claim his battered remains
that he would not be counted among the countless
who were stolen by these men
from their homes,
streets
fields
huts
and disappeared as if they were never born
except that they now float like a rotting corpse would on water
on the memory of the people;
steve knew this
he had to, he was a bright boy
there was a funeral in kingwilliamstown

there have been many many funerals in my country
funerals
of bright babies
whose fresh and young blood was spilled in the streets
by fire-power of God's children
there are commemorations all over the world
of my countrymen
some of whom fought and lost
some fell defenceless
we in my country and fell and keep fighting
ask blood river
and soweto will answer
that:

> school children took to the street one day. there
> will never be another soweto. nor, south africa.
> there are many kinds of deaths, and soweto knows
> them all, south africa too, and southern africa. you
> cannot kill children like cattle and then hope that
> guns are a monopoly. we were born like everybody
> else, and like everybody else, we know when it is
> too late or, to put it another way, when there is
> nothing any longer to lose. we made love in strange
> places: ghettoes, that is, we gave birth in these
> holes. we learnt from the pain and sorrow of
> having lost our children to so many and such cruel
> deaths as malnutrition or murder or sadness even
> dying while throwing spears or stones and being
> shot dead. we can now say, while we claim our land
> and die in the process: our history is a culture of
> resistance.

ask southern africa
mozambique
angola
zimbabwe
which we read while some men believe in god
and we know trouble
and say so, by scattering bloody milestones in places
where nobody would ever intend to die
since the types of deaths which are died in these places
ask us the price of liberation
and we ask ourselves nothing nice now
and south africa answers:

> europe took it from us, we fought and lost. the
> wheel kept spinning, slowly at first, whipping, as it
> spun us into position: landless, into mines.
> factories. tribes. race. ignorance. poverty. cogs of a
> machine, whose wheel spins and spins, ejects:
> insane, sick, ignorant, poor men and women,
> whose children were now caught, in a fast spinning
> wheel, which whipped off more and more land-
> less, uneducated, poor people, bloody, fast, insane.

        the wheel keeps spinning and spinning. it spins. had
        spun, and the union of south africa was born,
        whipping thousands and millions of landless, under-
        paid, ill-educated, men and women who build
        cities day and night and rest in ghettoes, if they
        ever do, poor, playing hide and seek with all types
        of deaths.
yes —
we did make distances
from blood river
to sharpeville to soweto
we know now
that oppression has been unmasked and will act true to our expectations
we ask, why oppress us
to exploit us
why exploit us
and now we learn and that is because we are born so that we should live,
that the chain must be broken
whatever the fuck this chain was made for:
        days go by like everyday, we bury the dead who
        died cruel and strange deaths. yet, like we said,
        memory is like water which shores up rotten
        corpses.
yet,
that isn't enough
memories don't break chains
nor does dying like dogs or cattle
or throwing stones and bricks at mad armed men
nor do lies at the U.N., or anywhere else.
my people, tell me:
what does, what breaks the chains?

the bright eye of the night keeps whispering and whispering
when it paves and pages the clouds
it is knowledgeable about hideous nights
when it winks and winks like that and the stars keep whistling
it will see us one day
when children, mad at us, will spit and kick us in public
they had their trouble; they ask us about the love we made so that they
        could be born
for what?
soweto?
please, can someone, my countrymen, say a word of wisdom
we need the truth not fiction
when we ask why;
we need to hear words
which, if the lips which make them, do tremble
they do so only because they know
they understand the perilous billows of our country which we've learnt
        how to ride

not because they fear our stare
or they are angry because we do not believe the report.
alas —
time has run out:
    too much blood has been spilled. please my
    countrymen, can someone say a word of wisdom.
    it is too late. blood, no matter how little of it, when
    it spills, spills on the brain — on the memory of a
    nation — it is as if the sea floods the earth, the
    lights go out. mad hounds howl in the dark; ah,
    now we've become familiar with horror. the heart
    of our country, when it makes its pulse, ticking
    time, wounds us. my countrymen, can someone,
    who understands that it is now too late, who
    knows that exploitation and oppression are brains
    which, being insane, only know how to make
    violence; can someone teach us how to mount the
    wound, and fight.
time has run out —
period.

                              (1980)

Sipho Sepamla

To Whom It May Concern

Bearer
Bare of everything but particulars
Is a Bantu
The language of a people in southern Africa
He seeks to proceed from here to there
Please pass him on
Subject to these particulars
He lives
Subject to the provisions
Of the Urban Natives Act of 1925
Amended often
To update it to his sophistication
Subject to the provisions of the said Act
He may roam freely within a prescribed area
Free only from the anxiety of conscription
In terms of the Abolition of Passes Act
A latter-day amendment
In keeping with moon-age naming
Bearer's designation is Reference number 417181
And (he) acquires a niche in the said area
As a temporary sojourner
To which he must betake himself
At all times
When his services are dispensed with for the day
As a permanent measure of law and order
Please note
The remains of R/N 417181
Will be laid to rest in peace
On a plot
Set aside for Methodist Xhosas
A measure also adopted
At the express request of the Bantu
In anticipation of any faction fight
Before the Day of Judgement.
                              (1975)

Come Duze Baby

Hela baby!
Zwakala daarso
Of hoe sê ek?

Jy moet my notch
Kyk my mooi sweetie
Ek is nie een van hulle

120

Jy ken mos
Die Hillbrow type.

Hela Sisi!
Look sharp
Otherwise jy val
Met my 'M'
Jy val soos 'n sak kool.

Ek wil jou weedie
Of praat jy net met situations
Die manne met 'n ntanjana
Die Stetson oukies
Die Mpala-mpala outies
Wat jou rwa
Met Manyeledi
And Mgababa
Of hoe sê ek?

Baby jy's 'n washout
Hulle vang jou
Sluit jou toe
For Immorality
'Strue met my 'P'
Jy's 'n has-been.

Kyk, ek mca jou baby
Ek is serious
My hart maak shandies
Jy ken mos
Die downtown beat
Van Jimmy Smith se mojo.

Ek praat die real ding
Moenie dink
Ek wala-wala net stof
Ek wil jou cover
Ek wil jou smekana
Jy ken mos
Die movie-star ding.

Jy's my number one mbuzana
Die neneweet
Jy's my eie ding
Met my ma!

Baby come duze!
Come duze baby!

The Blues Is You in Me

When my heart pulsates a rhythm
off-beat with God's own scintillating pace
and I can trace only those thoughts
that mar the goodness of living with you
then I know I've got the blues for howling

> yeah I've been howling
> clouds have been muffling
> and the rain has come
> and washed away
> these blues of mine

> the blues is you in me

I want to say it louder now
I want to holler my thoughts now
for I never knew the blues until I met you

> the blues is you in me

the blues is the clicks of my tongue
agitated by the death I live

the blues is my father's squeals
every Friday in a week

> the blues is you in me
> I never knew the blues until I met you

the blues is the screeches of the censor's pen
as he scribbles lamentations on my sensitized pad
the blues is the shadow of a cop
dancing the Immorality Act jitterbug

the blues is the Group Areas Act and all its jive

the blues is the Bantu Education Act and its
   improvisations

> the blues is you in me
> I never knew the blues until I met you

the blues is people huddled on a bench
eating of their own thoughts

the blues is those many words said to repair
yesterdays felled again and again by today's promises

the blues is the long shadow I count
measured by moments dragging the sun

the blues is the ratting of my brother
for opportunities he gets which he ought to have had

      the blues is you in me
      I never knew the blues until I met you

I want to holler the how-long blues
because we are the blues people all
the whiteman bemoaning his burden
the blackman offloading the yoke

      the blues is you in me
      I never knew the blues until I met you.

I Tried to Say . . .

I tried to say hullo
above the heads of the
milling, rushing crowd
above the din of grinding gears
and belching trucks

I saw the grim clasping
of a brown paper parcel
and I knew you held
a clean white shirt and khaki trousers
stained with a drop of His blood

I saw the pain waiting
on your wrinkling, greying face
and I stayed a cry for him
because everybody knew
he stood for a certain calmness

Beyond the grasp of the grousing road gang
their agitated chanting
swinging on an emotional chord
I tried to say please forgive me

I would have said I make do
with such transparencies
as aspirins and other pain-killers
because some concrete slab that fingers skies
has turned the joys of living
into palpitations of the heart

Earlier I had stood like a member
of the herd
listening to the screams and pleas
of the preacher
on the steps of the City Hall
I saw those banners proclaiming
the Second Coming
to me they appeared
inverted urgings

For days I've pondered the reality
that lives with us
like the green of Lanky tufts of grass
whether to sit by the window
watching shadows turn to night
or make those little noises
that affirm our tilted existence

Double-Talk

I was here when the windswept dust dunes
rose in the streets
each footfall of sweatstained man standing up dust
and minedump clouds were rising into the air
galloping like an army of ghosts
tickling the ear with whispering sands
teeth grinding grit on dry tongues

Now that long concrete necks crane and
are craning so impetuously into God's den
straining steel muscles that they may glimmer
in the rising and setting sun
I've watched expectantly. Not in vain. For I have been
reading the message from the drums
a low-toned moan
that now rises into a delirious desperate cry
of forsaken purposes and discarded promises
ever said never seen

And so where I stand
I can barely hear people whisper
they hurry and they jostle
their voices a murmuring hum
over a huge enforced silence
while tattered heads have begun to nod
as if to say
it is all very well . . .

Statement: The Dodger

Hayi ke mos
This world inento zawo

This fellow-ndini ndithi-speak about
Ndimqhelile, I'm used to him ngaloo way
Yokumthi-see everyday on the street

He comes to me one day
You know nge-same way
Ka-I'll be alright tomorrow Jack
He says ndimthi-borrow i-five bob
Uzandithi-fixup on a Friday
Xa sithi-meet again on the way

Hayi man I don't give le nto i-second thought
Ndamthi-pity umntu kaThixo
Ngale ngqondo ka-blessed is he that gives
Ndathi rwaa i-five bob out of my pocket
Ndayithi give to him
Next thing I walk away

Two three weeks go by
Le chap ithe-disappear
Not a ghost sign of him anywhere

Ke what is five bob these days ze-cost of living
One can't even buy snuff ngaloo amount

One Saturday afternoon
Ndisathi-relax ne-friends of mine kwa-Mrs January
Yi-next door neighbour ka-Mrs May
We were doing woza-2 woza-4
I-session yamadoda ane-public opinion
In walks this fellow
Wagaleleka I tell you
Ndiphi by then
Kwa-Love and Peace
Andingxilanga ndiyashusha
Drunk as a sailor I tell you

I-fellow le he doesn't see me
Whether fair or foul I didn't know
Wathi esathi kwi-owner of the joint
One scotch here: Johnny Walker
I jumped up and said
Khawundincede buti ngalaa parcel

Hey!
Wathi esandithi-reply ngo-don't be funny

125

Ndathi-take five!
A helluva chap leyo

Women started to scream
Ndathi: take six!
A clap plus ndamthi-point nge-one finger

Everybody grabbed my hands

I told them straight
Le guy ithi-take advantage of me
Ithe-borrow five bob from me the other day long ago
Endithi-promise ukuyithi-return on a Friday
Soon soon
Now grass has grown under my feet

I don't like promises
Especially from people who drink whisky

Hayi ke mos
This world is real funny

Song of Mother and Child

Song of mother and child
singing for the man
whose beard grew grey
in search of gold

Oh! clash of cow-hide shields
spears clattering
into the limbo of symbols
see what birth has given
in time

O ashes of a father
entombed in the abyss of things
sing:

hay' hay' igoli igoli
hay' hay' igoli igoli

of widowed mothers
singing of the living dead
ageing men who nod so often
as if to say
the past must come back

Oh! where are the heroes
where are the heroes

126

that the child might lisp
names that might father sons-of-yield

hay'hay'igoli igoli
hay'hay' igoli igoli

of seeds scattered on sickly soils
the air fouled by indecisive acts
where men are put to flight
in the moist dawn
spirits of the dead floating about
in search of fellow-beings

Oh! igoli of white fleeting clouds
lifted as arms in supplication
collared by desperation
because there are no men here
only the act of gasping

hay'hay' igoli igoli
hay'hay' igoli igoli

of men long gone
who will come back dead

O spirits spew here and now
the shine of your gold
that we may live in times glittering
singing:

igoli igoli igoli

Soweto

I have watched you grow
like fermented dough
and now that you overflow the bowl
I'm witness to the panic you have wrought

you were born an afterthought
on the by-paths of highways
and have lived a foster child
whose wayward ways have broken hearts
the myths attending your name
have been spooks in the minds of many

your sons have been legendaries
whose strength of character
has been a cause of pride

you have been a bad dream
which has gnawed at the conscience of some
until averted eyes looked on
at the teeming mass of beings

there have been times
the incisions on your ear-lobes were misread
and those on your wrists abused
there have been times
the song from a thousand of your voices
was heard as a discord
and the dance of a million of your feet
was said to be off the beat

on your neck was placed a yoke of laws
which has tried to strangle your life
and once you strained muscles
to shake off the restraints
a great roar went up abroad

I love you Soweto
I've done so long before
the summer swallow deserted you
I have bemoaned the smell of death
hanging on your other neck like an albatross
I have hated the stench of your blood
blood made to flow in every street

but I have taken courage
in the thought that
those who mother your back
will carry on with the job
of building anew
a body of being
from the ashes in the ground

Mafika Gwala

Kwela-Ride

Dompas!
I looked back
Dompas!
I went through my pockets
Not there.

They bit into my flesh (handcuffs).

Came the kwela-kwela
We crawled in.
The young men sang.
In that dark moment

It all became familiar.

One Small Boy Longs for Summer

(for Bill Naughton)

The kettle hisses
Mother moves about the kitchen
sliding from corner to corner.
The fire from the stove
pierces into the marrow.
And mother pushing towards the stove
warns of the steam.
My young brother, Thamu, jerks my arm
violently: Stop leaning on me, your elbow
has sunk into my thigh.
      Apology
         I wasn't aware.

The kettle sings
      Some distant far-away song?
Mother picks it up
with an almost tender care.
Sets me thinking of a war-picture
The actor carefully setting the charge
and smiling all the time
        I'll also be a soldier
when I'm old - why, Uncle Shoba was one.
Father drops the paper on the table
He comes to join us
        — staring coldly round.
It's no frown really,
But he's grinding his jaws.

Maybe it's the July
Handicap.

The kettle purrs now
Steam is escaping; it kisses the ceiling
and vanishes. Mother is pouring the violent waters
into the coffee-jug. Coffee
Yes, I need some coffee — a mug of hot coffee
Very rousing.
We can't play outside — I must not go, I know
          How we danced in the rain. We are so tired
of the winter: It's so dingy outside.
We can't play inside — I'm so tied up.
It's so boring, I feel like bursting into
a cracking laughter; but father
he'll go mad.
It's so steamy inside
I feel I could bite the walls down.
If only it makes the winter pass.

We Lie under Tall Gum-Trees

We lie under tall gum-trees
hidden from the moonlight,
the stars and the silvery summer clouds.
In the thick shadows of tall gum-trees.

Mosquitoes hover round
and above us.
Swarming from the black swamps
of a pulp factory nearby
—like jetbombers blackening the Vietnam skies.
And as we spiralled
towards awareness
they bit us.
First you.
Then me.

Now, no more a virgin
You have tasted
the painful joy of love.

The Bangalala

Calm was all he wanted
(So he told his wife,
And the people who questioned him).
Shifty-shafty he trudged
The township night

To curb the rising tsotsi crime
With his beer-swelled stomach that bulged.

It continued
Until a sixteen-year-old girl
Came and abandoned a small baby
On the sofa in his house
Telling the shocked wife:
'A parcel for your husband!'
And she walked out.
That evening he came home staggering drunk.

Night Party

Saturday evening
Berea Road Station
the 1044's long been gone.
By the time
I touch Mpumalanga
at Zero-One-Thirty Hour
got to zwakala
into this wholenight gig;
Winwood & Capaldi
create Traffic on cellophane
in a world
already bored
with riches and hoboes.
the same vile wealth
that drugged Jimi Hendrix
out of Life,
the same nourished want
that starved the sax bit
of Charlie 'Bird' Parker
to his grave.
By break of Sunday's dawn
with scanted
      crooked
chimney smokes
straightening me home
the eagles have already
flown in.

The Children of Nonti

Nonti Nzimande died long, long ago
Yet his children still live.
Generation after generation, they live on;
Death comes to the children of Nonti

And the children of Nonti cry but won't panic
And there is survival in the children of Nonti.

Poverty swoops its deathly wings. But tough,
strong and witty are the children of Nonti.
The wet rains fall. The roads become like
the marshed rice paddies of the Far East;
And on these desolate roads there is song
Song in the Black voices of the children of Nonti.

Someone marries
The bride does not hide her face under the veil;
The maidens dance near the kraal
Dance before the 'make it be merry' eyes
of the elders. The elders joshing it
on their young days.
There is still free laughter
in the children of Nonti.

An ox drops to the earth, then another;
Knives run into the meat. Making the feast
to be bloodfilled with Life.
The old, the dead, are brought into the Present
of continuous nature in the children of Nonti.
Got to be a respecting with the children of Nonti.

When a daughter has brought shame
The women show anger; not wrath.
And the illegitimate born is one of
the family.
When a son is charged by the white law
The children of Nonti bring their heads together
In a bid to free one of the children of Nonti.

There are no sixes and nines be one
with the children of Nonti. Truth is truth
and lies are lies amongst the children of Nonti.
For when summer takes its place after the winter
The children of Nonti rejoice
and call it proof of Truth
Truth reigns amongst the children of Nonti.

Sometimes a son rises above the others
of the children of Nonti. He explains the workings
and the trappings of white thinking.
The elders debate;
And add to their abounding knowledge
of black experience.
The son is still one of the black children of Nonti
For there is oneness in the children of Nonti.

And later, later when the sun
is like forever down;
Later when the dark rules
above the light of Truth
The black children of Nonti will rise and speak.
They will speak of the time
when Nonti lived in peace with his children;
Of the times when age did not count
above experience. The children of Nonti will stand
their grounds in the way that Nonti speared his foes
to free his black brothers from death and woes;
They shall fight with the tightened grip
of a cornered pard. For they shall be knowing that
Nothing is more vital than standing up
For the Truths that Nonti lived for.
Then there shall be Freedom in that stand
by the children of Nonti.
Truthful tales shall be told
Of how the children of Nonti pushed their will;
And continued to live by the peace
The peace that Nonti once taught to them.

Food for the Couple

He hadn't gone to the wedding ceremony
at the local parish.
I asked him why.
'Man, it's my brother Sitha,' he started.
'He courted her for three years
They went steady for four years.
They quarrelled, he went to Jo'burg
And swore he didn't want her
There were brighter girls there —
What was she but an old maid?
Away he went for five years.
Until he heard she was marrying
this morning her former highschoolday teacher
— his arch rival.
He came back last night — almost greying all over.
And a damned stupid thing he did
this morning. He hanged himself
— in the lavatory.'

Getting off the Ride

I
I get off the bus ride
after long standing
listening to black voices
that obliviate the traffic noises;
A billboard overwhelms me,
Like an ugly plastic monster with fiercy eyes
it tells me what canned drink
will be good enough to quench my thirst;
I eye-mock the plastic arrogance
'Cos I know, shit, I know
I'm being taken for a ride.

II
Past this Patel's shop
The hustling efforts of these youngsters
almost urge me into seriously viewing
their imitation wrist watches,
When I know they are wanting to drain me
of the few Rands I'm still left with —
So's their brothers can get to the top drop;
And me to go on entering shops
— throwing my last Rands each time;
Ya, I know I'm being taken for a ride.

III
At the cinema house
the big poster poses a bigcrowd drawer,
I slide into the darkness;
The still blackness
is nothing but inverted blackness
cast upon imposed darkness;
I throw my eyes on the screen . . .
. . . then the long watch.
I walk out worse off,
Worse than when I mooched in;
Movies can be made to fast sell the mind
(an old warning in the family quips) like
the inflation coin at the tourist bazaar.
Again I know I've been taken for a ride.

IV
My boots jar me
as I take the corner off Grey Street
Into Victoria's busy, buzzy Victoria
Beesy Victoria's market area.
Some black mamas kneeling
their hands on the sidewalk

their second-hand clothes before them,
They kneel as if in prayer.
A white hippie bums towards them
with what shapes into a pair of
fawn corduroy jeans:
'They are fishbottomed', the aunt tilts
the deal. The seller hooks a feigned smile
with his cagey chin,
Looks like both have no choice
So the limp deal is sealed.
With unease the hippie moves off
You'd swear he's left a bomb to detonate;
I radar his moves
whilst yarning my eyes onto the mama,
the mama still on that solemn kneel
that's accompanied by sombre looks
from close range.
Where's that hippish fixer?
Into the market lanes for a blow-up;
And the black mama to scrounge a sale
after a wash of these sweaty pants
that can only be bought by some black brother
whose boss won't give him enough to afford
a pair of decent trousers.
And again I know I'm being taken for a ride.

V
I know this ride bloody well.
I'm from those squatted mothers
Those squatted mothers in the draughty air;
Those mothers selling handouts,
Those mothers selling fruits,
Those mothers selling vegetables,
Those mothers selling till dusk
in the dusty streets of Clermont, Thembisa,
Alex, Galeshewe, Dimbaza, Pietersburg.
Those mothers in dusty and tearful streets
that are found in Stanger, Mandeni, Empangeni
Hammarsdale, Mabopane, Machibisa, Soweto.
I'm one of the sons of those black mamas,
Was brought up in those dust streets;
I'm the black mama's son who vomits
on the doorstep of his shack home, pissed with
concoction. Because his world and the world
in town are as separate as the mountain ranges
and the deep sea.
I'm the naked boy
running down a muddy road,
the rain pouring bleatingly
in Verulam's Mission Station;

With the removal trucks brawling for starts
Starts leading to some stifling redbricked
ghetto of four-roomed houses at Ntuzuma.
I'm the pipeskyf pulling cat
standing in the passage behind Ndlovu's barbershop
Making dreams and dreams
Dreaming makes and makes;
Dreaming, making and making, dreaming
with poetry and drama scripts
rotting under mats
or being eaten by the rats.
I'm the staggering cat on Saturday morning's
West Street. The cat whose shattered hopes
were bottled up in beers, cane, vodka;
Hopes shattered by a system that once offered
liquor to 'Exempted Natives' only.
I'm the bitter son leaning against the lamp post
Not wishing to go to school
where his elder brother spent years, wasted years
at school wanting to be white; only to end as
messenger boy.
I'm the skollie who's thrown himself
out of a fast moving train
Just to avoid blows, kicks and the hole.
I'm one of the surviving children of Sharpeville
Whose black mothers spelled it out in blood.
I'm the skhotheni who confronts devil-eyed cops
down Durban's Grey Street . . .
Since he's got no way to go out.
I'm the young tsotsi found murdered in a donga
in the unlit streets of Edendale, Mdantsane.

VI
I'm the puzzled student
burning to make head and tail of Aristotle
because he hasn't heard of the buried
Kingdom of Benin or the Zimbabwe Empire,
The student who is swotting himself to madness
striving for universal truths made untrue.
I'm the black South African exile who has come
across a coughing drunk nursing his tuberculosis
on a New York pavement and remembered
he's not free.
I'm the black newspaper vendor
standing on the street corner 2 o'clock
in the morning of Sunday,
Distributing news to those night life crazy
nice-timers who will one day come into knocks
with the real news.
I'm the youthful Black with hopes of life
standing on file queue for a job
at the local chief's kraal,

This chief who has let himself and his people
into some confused Bantustan kaak
Where there's bare soil, rocks and cracking cakes
of rondavel mudbricks.
I'm the lonely poet
who trudges the township's ghetto passages
pursuing the light,
The light that can only come through a totality
of change:
Change in minds, change
Change in social standings, change
Change in means of living, change
Change in dreams and hopes, change
          Dreams and hopes that are Black
          Dreams and hopes where games end
          Dreams where there's end to man's
creation of gas chambers and concentration camps.
I'm the Africa Kwela instrumentalist whose notes
profess change.

VII
They say the Black Ghost is weak
That it is feeble
and cannot go the distance.
I say that's their wishful thinking:
The Black Ghost outmanoeuvres the wiles of Raleigh
on treacherous seas,
The ghost that steamed South Pacific trains
to Florida after Tres Castillos was not black;
Which ghost spurned the wiles of Rhodes,
Rhodes treating Black hospitality as scraps
of paper?
No, I know the Black Ghost.
It has led to many victories
In the pitch darkness of dispossession;
I can sit back and watch the screen
of Black Thoughts
In which Black success is focused.
I may not have seen Spartacus, Attila
or the Maccabee brothers for that score;
I also did not see Shaka, the Kofikarikari
or Mshweshwe, Bhambatha, for another score;
And down to those Black youths with guns
in the streets of Watts, Harlem, Oakland.
The people of Guinea-Bissau shed their tears
for Cabral with the muzzles of their guns.
Sharpeville's Black Ghost haunts all racists,
Urges the Black people forward.
I live with this Ghost.
I've come to love this Ghost.
I live with the Black Ghost

When I'm dumped in soulless structures
From Windhoek to Pretoria to Pietersburg
From Gugulethu to Makhutha to Ngwelezana;
Where I'm denied understanding
according to statutes of ethnic rule;
My brothers who are caged in prisons
My brothers waiting in the dark street corners
My brothers sent to mental asylums
My brothers forced into exile
My brothers who bullshit me for a Rand
My brothers who dream of a Ford Mustang
          when they've gone to bed on empty stomachs
My brothers who'll sell their fellow brothers
          when they've lost the key to survival
My brothers who'll roll their fathers on
          Friday night.
Yes, I'm made to feel motherless, fatherless, shitless
Me with enough shit in my guts to blackshit
          any officiated shit,
Me wishing for a gun
When I know some pig will wish to collar me
for the 3-Star knife I've bought at the shop
down the street.

VIII
I hate this ride.
When I know Dudu Pukwana's horn
is blowing winter out of London's black crowds;
I hate this ride.
When I dance to Miriam Makeba
Miriam Makeba's 'Jol'iinkomo' that brings back
the proud and angry past of my ancestors
by whom tribe did not be taken for nation;
I hate this ride.
When I learn no Latin from faked classics
When 2 x 2 economics shows me it's part of the
          trick — teaching me how to starve
When Coca Cola, Pepsi Cola ads, all the sweet things
          are giving me wind in the belly;
I ask again, what is Black?
Black is when you get off the ride.
Black is point of self realization
Black is point of new reason
Black is point of: NO NATIONAL DECEPTION!
Black is point of determined stand
Black is point TO BE or NOT TO BE for blacks
Black is point of RIGHT ON!
Black is energetic release from the shackles of Kaffir, Bantu, non-white.
Sometimes there's a fall
when brother gets off the ride,
And the fall hurts;

138

A fall is a hurt to every black brother.
Then I smell the jungle
I get the natural smell of the untamed jungle;
I'm with the mamba
I learn to understand the mamba
I become a khunga-khunga man
I'm with the Black Ghost of the skom jungle
I get the smell of phuthu in a ghetto kitchen
The ghetto, a jungle I'm learning to know
I hear the sound of African drums beating
to freedom songs;
And the sound of the Voice come:
            Khunga, Khunga!
        Untshu, Untshu!
                ' Funtu, Funtu!
        Shundu, Shundu!!
            Sinki, Sinki!
                    Mojo, Mojo!
O-m! O--o--m! O----hhhhhhhhhhmmmm!!!
The voice speaks:
'I'm the Voice that moves with the Black Thunder
I'm the Wrath of the Moment
I strike swift and sure
I shout in the West and come from the East
I fight running battles with enemy gods
        in the black clouds
I'm the watersnake amongst watersnakes
        and fish amongst fish
I throw missiles that outspace the SAM
I leave in stealth
        and return in Black anger.
O---m! Ohhh---mmmm! O----hhhhhhmmmmmmmmm!!!'

                                    (1977)

Post-Soweto
(1976 – Present Day)

Farouk Asvat

Possibilities for a Man Hunted by SBs

There's one of two possibilities
Either they find you or they don't
If they don't it's ok
But if they find you
There's one of two possibilities
Either they let you go or they ban you
If they let you go it's ok
But if they ban you
There's one of two possibilities
Either you break your ban or you don't
If you don't it's ok
But if you break your ban
There's one of two possibilities
Either they find out or they don't
If they don't it's ok
But if they find out
There's one of two possibilities
Either they find you guilty or not guilty
If they find you not guilty it's ok
But if they find you guilty
There's one of two possibilities
Either they suspend your sentence or they jail you
If they suspend your sentence it's ok
But if they jail you
There's one of two possibilities
Either they release you
Or you fall from the tenth floor

Shabbir Banoobhai

the morning caught me

the morning caught me
reaching
for the sky

in shafts of light
i said
i'd travel home

in fire
cleanse
my song

chastened
i'd etch my want
deep in the heart of god

oh what lack of love
has caught me
lingering here

in a land where night
must come
to wash me black again

the border

the border

is as far
as the black man
who walks alongside you

as secure
as your door
against the unwanted knock

for my father

for my father

days
    when you roughshod your way
through town and village and countryside

when your father bought the radio
    he had promised so long ago
and the laughter of the child rippled in his eyes

when the boy cracked the whip of exuberance
    and the mother stayed quiet
for she knew he was young

when the man emerged
    from the hideout of the boy
and caught the blast of life on his face

when the man spat on his hands
    and ploughed the land
and watched the sky for rain

when wife and child
    sat by his side
and lit the fire that was once his pride

nights
    when the light of a full, full moon
seemed dull against your bright, white face

when we still hoped
    held your hand
tried to breathe our strength into you

when you faltered at last
    slipped from our grasp
lost your will in the hills

Achmat Dangor

The Voices that are Dead

I
There is a silence
upon the river tonight.
No great floods of song
flow out into the darkness,
our voices are dead.

And the midnight moon
White and cold
over the ashen streets
reveals nothing but shadows
fleeing from one darkness
to the next.

Mattera, Mohapi, Mathe,
Nortje, Nakasa
and you Brutus,
names and voices
that few remember.

II
Oh, my brothers,
poets of the earth
who ripped handfuls
of flesh from the land
as salt for the tears
in your songs.
And today,
like black madrigals,
sing with gilded voices
in the great white halls,
at the soirees
of a people whose souls
are famished.

And you are their final,
sad repast,
whom they sit down to sup
with the now uncertain air
of imperial ceremony.

Oh, my brothers —
you too are dead,
your voices rage barrenly

within the august halls
of the doomed,

but are not heard
by the cowherd who treads
his unknowing peace,
not is it heard
in the ashen townships
where soon your memory
will flit unlovingly
from one darkness to the next.

III
Yet, I can write of hope,
though the voice I hear
in the icy dawn
is still frail and tremulous,
and the mists are a portend
of a familiar and savage storm.

I can sing a hymn
to the glory of my land,
from the ashes something stirs,
new voices are being heard.

I can look with love
at the harsh landscape
pockmarked by ghettoes.
In the dust and the dirt
new voices sing new songs.

Yet still the morning rises
as if drenched in blood.
Oh Lord, save them
from the gunfire
and the jackboot.

Fhazel Johennesse

the african pot

it is round and fat and squat
it has no handle and the rim has no spout
at first it seems as if the colours have
no coordination and no rhythm
the yellow and brown stripes circle
the pot in quick diagonals

i puzzle over the absence of the handle
and then suddenly i think of a young woman
wearing beads walking to a river with
the pot gracefully balanced on her head

and then the colours begin to rhyme
yellow zigzagging around the top
makes me think of harvest time   of golden corn
of dances around an autumn fire   of ripe fruit
and of men drinking homebrewed beer

and as i stroke the brown
i can almost feel the full earth between
my fingers   earth that echoes the thunderous
stamp of warriors going to war   .earth that
offers base accompaniment to dancing feet
i can almost see an ox pulling a plough
steered by a man of infinite patience
making ordered rows of upturned loam

the maker made this pot
with a song in his heart
and a vision in his eyes
lifting it up i can almost hear
him say
        i am man
        life is but clay in my hands
        creation is at my fingertips

for george masoka

they say you were found like that
your face all bashed in and pulpy
and your chest full of gaping holes
draped over the steering wheel
crumpled small and pathetic
but i cannot picture you like that
silent and bloody with flies buzzing around you

and it is strange that you should die that way
with knives pumping up and down
on your chest draining all your blood
funny you should die that way
when these days people are either
being shot in riots or hung in cells
and you get battered and stabbed in your car
i know you would have preferred another
death some other way
a death less filled with violence
and question marks
maybe dying on your bed wheezing
with age and mellow with satisfaction
i mourn your death
no i regret   i resent it
why you
but yet i know it is pointless to ask
why you were chosen to wear a mask of horror
and a halo of blood
i miss you anyway
i miss your quiet voice
even if you did talk rot sometimes
and your eyes i miss them
the way they shone when
bright with beer
and if there is rest in death
i hope you find it
i don't know why
but your death makes me
feel older not wiser
just older

the taxi driver

his route curves and winds
between the township bus stop
and the city the legend
    2nd class taxi
painted discreetly on his car

as he charges with his full load
he knows which traffic cops to smile at
he sits in a corner holding
the steering wheel at an angle
a golf cap perched on his head
a pair of the darkest sunglasses
give him a look of supreme control
    but his hands are clammy

and i know his only certainty
is the next forty cents

149

thinking about a white christmas

overseas they have white christmas
snow burying everything in sight
and making it all seem soft and lovely
while down here in the south
christmas is celebrated in driving heat
i try to connect snow and christmas
i fail and then i laugh
because as i think about it
i realise that christmas down here
is really a very white affair

my township sunset

when the sun begins to melt just above the
horizon and the clouds disappear to undress
the stars i'll squat against a corroded
washline pole and take a deep breath
sigh and breathe again

i always enjoy these dusk solitudes
these languid cigarettes and floating smoke
rings and i'll note with surprise how content
the overflowing dustbin looks
but the zenith of my township sunset is when
the swallows begin to chase the retreating light
the sudden dip smooth bank and frenzied darting
is a ballet at high speed

but just as the last drop of sunlight
dribbles below the skyline my sunset will
reach its nadir and i'll flick my
cigarette but angrily because it is then
that my graceful ballerinas become
sneering devils flitting to a
tune with words by langenhoven

The Dying Ground
(It is known that elephants, when sensing that death is near,
walk for thousands of miles to a special 'dying ground'
where they lay themselves down without food or drink until they
die . . .)

The elephants came
and brought with them
a crookery of God
and brotherhood,
took our verdant land
with gunpowder and psalms
and proclaimed a covenant
in his name.

Today, the fetters bite deeper
cruelty is resolute,
genocide defined.

Beyond Azania,
black children eat manhood
from bloody pots
and freedom is sown
with the seeds of valiant men
The harvest is bitter for the settlers and now,
the last exodus gathers frenzy.

The trail points Southward
to the last outpost
(a haven to their whiteness).

And like elephants,
sensing the final hour
they hurry to the sacred sand
(our conquered land)

But let them come
O let the white elephants draw near!

What would be their refuge
Will yet become
Their Dying Ground . . .

*pen name

Ingoapele Madingoane

from black trial

man the coward
has disowned himself
the rights given to him
by nature
and adopted the fake romance
of self

how i hate the deceitful paradise
that man lives within
and the selfish way he now handles my life

i blew my horn to raise the alarm
and he told me that's no right way
to save us both
i beat the drum
and he loosened the cowhide to stifle the beat
so i left him and wandered alone
in the black forest and asked myself
what in fact does man want

i resigned from paradise
and went back home to africa
in search of my image
to dig up the roots
and burn incense
to strengthen my stand
speaking to my ancestors
in the ancient language of mankind
i heard the spirits talk back to me
i felt my soul astir as they led me
all the way from a black trial
into the land of sunshine and peace
i heard them say
leap high deprived soul
move faster than yesteryear
and climb the freedom wagon
go man go
blackman go

don't crawl to your future
you are bound to be brave
reach your goal blackman
stand up man   stand up and
go man go
blackman go

drag it off brother man
off your back   it ain't yours
break this damn sucker's chain
drop the burden from your shoulders
move on   brother go
go man go
blackman go

leap higher deprived son
jump the lagoon of dark despair
walk to the point of salvation
blow the horn   raise the alarm
beat the drum and let them dance
go man go
blackman go

go man go
blackman go
turn a new leaf
date this creation
scribble on the soil
a good reflection
up off your backside
and
go man go
blackman go

i talk about me
i am africa
i am the blazing desert yonder
a tall proud grain amidst the sand
egypt my head   the nile my oasis
flow on nile   flow on my life blood
i talk about me
i am africa
i am man
ogun's image
made from the soil
abibiman
thus
i talk about me
for
i am africa

hide and seek i lived
on savanna grasslands
talking freedom
eating salvation
sleeping courage
and

153

dreaming liberation
for the african soil
thus
i talk about man
i talk about me
for
I am africa

jambo i said as i greeted my father
babari   mzuri sana   as he nodded in agreement
a sign of love and admiration
wewe unatoka wapi he asked me
this question the ageing poor man
not aware he was talking to his long lost son
mimi ninatoka nchini kwa africa kusine
kule kwa azania
kwanini wewe umefika hapa
i said *babu nimekuja kuwona ninyi*
in africa the land of your sons
are you in africa   is that you *mwana*
he asked
yes babu   it is me your son
usema nini he asked me again
hapana maneno i answered
he said
        hail *ogun*
        hail *abibiman*
        land of my sons
        sons of my soil
        bed of my roots
        roots of man
        man   son of africa
        i want you
        back
        back home in africa
        when i lost you
        you were a virgin rich with love
        until they split your loins
        eagle spread and raped you all
        within three centuries
        when they boasted their manhood and
        you abandoned their first child
        in the remote trans
        kei
        oh child   land of my sons
        come back home to africa
come back home azania my child
give up your prodigal life
don't go flirting again
maybe in *bophutamokete*
this time

154

come child
land of my sons
sons of the soil
bed of my roots
roots of man
man   son of africa
peace in africa will be restored
not because man in africa is black but
because he's suffered under the common enemy
for we in africa will not bring colour
between man and reality

so when I say that don't think
politics will be brought into art
for art is in its own
right above politics   bear in mind
brother whatever you do which is not harmful
to the community
has an artistic message of use to the society
and yourself
remember
africa's pride can be expressed in many ways
your face with music
            your pain with music
                    your joy with music
and of course your artistic gift
is as important as your presence
wherever the clan gathers so
stick to them brother because
even man is no man without
the structure of his culture
            so beautifully created
            that black natural gift
            from the mould of the african womb
            pity the day it rots
            in the traditional african tomb

it has been my wish and still is my wish
that   whatever happens between me and africa   when we
                                    part ways
it will not be through cowardice   or should i say
betrayal of my beloved fatherland

i would be glad if i could be buried like a true african
of african definition
            when i take my soul
            to its destination
            when the gong of departure
            reaches my eardrum
            and the cloud of death dominates my eye

wrap me safely
with the hide of an african ox
i will be glad
deliver me to the ancestral village
cast no flowers on my soil
i am an african   as for beauty
i never had a chance to admire it 'cause
africa was not free
i will join the masses that went before me
and as one we shall fight
the ancestral war until justice
is done

                    (1979)

Albert G.T.K. Malikongwa

A Protest from a Bushman

I
This is my native land
My real native land
I know every tree and bush by its name
I care not that I am poor
I have lived in this land
And hunted all over these mountains
And looked at the skies
And wondered how the stars
And the moon and the sun
The rainbow and the milky way
Rush from day to day like busy people.

I have enjoyed this life
The light in the stars
The lilt in the music or songs
The joy in the flowers
The plumage in the birds
The charm in women's breasts
The inward warmth and rich vitality
The distant music of cowbells
All these lightened the burden of my sorrows
I have nothing outside this body
I have neither a house nor property
I roamed where I liked
And hunted wherever I chose.

I have enjoyed the bounce of youth
And stayed wherever I chose
I have danced in the sun
I have danced in the wind
I have danced around the fire place
But now and I say now
There is a swelling crescendo of sorrow
That makes goose pimples on my body
I live in sick apprehension
Freedom is gone
Life is tremulous like
A drop of water on a mophani leaf.

The talk is bushman everywhere
I am called a nobody
A race of rugged filthy people
Who cannot clean their floors
Whose blanket is the fire
Who spit and sneeze freely everywhere

Whose bodies smell of root ointment
Or like a cowhide soaked in the river water
My countrymen call me names
I am torn between life and death
Propped between freedom and slavery
I am almost like a wandering ghost

My tears glide in pairs down my cheeks
My hands shake because of old age
Sometimes I am struck with a horse whip
I am no more than a refugee
A loafer they say yet others loaf too
Whilst other men work
It is true I do not worry for lunch
As birds do not worry about theirs too
My countrymen eat, drink and laugh
They live in beautiful houses
My life is tremulous like
A drop of water on a mophani leaf.

I and my fellow men and women
Sleep under trees or in caves
Or on the open ground
Or around the open fire place
We starve and die of thirst
The finest part of our rich land is gone
We live in these dry and sandy hot deserts
We can no longer hunt freely
Life is a scourge, a curse
It is tremulous like
A water drop on a mophani leaf.

II
Man has become an intruder,
A puzzler, unstable, a sick being
A mafia to me and my brothers
Dispossessed am I of my land
Barbed wire do I see all over
The austerity of human laws do I feel
I bow down to red tape
I frown on the insensitivity of my countrymen
And on those that paraphrase my plight and my life
And with plethora of questions and stories
Donate bushmen paintings
To foreign museums and archives
To boost the coffers of selfish men
Life is tremulous like
a drop of water on a mophani leaf.

My countryman has become an intruder,
A puzzler, unstable, lured by the fetters

158

Of a civilization he does not understand
Hungrier, ever grabbing and balkanizing my land
Shackling it with iron and cement bridges
Wounding, burrowing holes into its river bed.
This land was once my private garden
Whereon I hunted as I pleased
And enjoyed the free kiss of the breeze
Bushman am I
Bushman in the blood
Bushman in the heart
My land is gone
Life is tremulous like
A drop of water on a mophani leaf.

I frown on the insensitivity of my countrymen
And on those who paraphrase my plight and my life
Into parables of ifs and perhapses
The erosive action of man's intransigence
Outshines the prudence of honest men
And man is now at variance with himself,
With his fellow men, and is forever grabbing.
These are the dynamics of a sick society
The austerity of human laws do I feel
No more do I enjoy the free laughter of the wind
No more do I enjoy the ferocity of lightning
No more do I enjoy the comforts of bushman medicine
This is tabooed
Life is tremulous like
A drop of water on a mophani leaf.

Senzo Malinga

At War with the Preacherman

My armful of goat skins
Captures the eyes of the preacherman;
I meet him on the shop verandah.
He tells me I have to change
my evil ways;
I go home cursing,
Declaring war against the preacherman.

Later he comes to my place
Accuses me of deflecting people
from the right way to Heaven;
I in turn call on my gods
To deliver their godly anger
upon this insolent preacherman;
For I do not live
That I may go to Heaven,
But that I may have supper tonight.

Themba ka Miya

The Question

We sat in patches of doom
        Discussing Eternity
All victimised by the question why

Why is Time the undisputed ruler
Why Time rules the minds of madness
Why Time rules from the womb to the tomb
Time that stretches the nerves of my past and cracks the skull of my
        future
Time, Time, Time!
You struck your hateful gong
        and hurried the City typist
        for her date with Adam
Who accepted the apple without dispute
        that gave birth to a man/child
Who was swallowed by a slimy polluted
        stream of a life system,

Involved without choice
We saw him reared in an existence of filth
We saw his body smeared in dung of extortion
We saw him listed on a tableau written in his own blood
We saw him in a world painted white, sucking from a love-starved
     system — caressing the doom of domination
We saw them bashing up his skull
        and eating his brains and imagination
        Symbol of Capitalism
We saw him trying to laugh only to end up sobbing
        At 16 he went and lost his name for a number
        At No. 80 Albert Str.
Who lamented in chains protest in his bondage and thereafter gave
        unopposed his gift of hate back handing to the unsociable
        society
Who was taught the pros and cons of turning the other cheek to the
        holy spirits bottled for Doornkop Cemetery (Pty) Limited
Who rushed to beg for manhood to reach the havens of ten rand a week,
        brandishing a flickering torch, chasing an evasive shadow of
        hope
Who was seen munching pig style, the vomit left-overs purchased at a
        'Whites Only' restaurant while sitting on the pavement of
        highway Jo'burg
Who turned to church and was told God is away on holiday
Who turned to surrender to the bantustans and was seen holding a
        baby dying of malnutrition
Who hung on until they told him that the cow did jump over the
  moon

Who turned to SASO and was told, 'Black man you are on your own'
Who turned to himself and saw human excrement and ended
        concluding the world is a prison
Who was later arrested crying, and charged with section 6
Who was seen in racist farms dressed to kill in potato sacks, his back
        bleeding from the whip of hate
Who walked down the withering limbs of his last discarded house
        and was later seen brandishing an okapi in soul-destroying
        Soweto
Whose father followed him into grandfather night trying to tell him
        what Time it was
        He followed as he watched helplessly his son's youth dribbling
        away as he staff-rode the soul train towards ancestral damnation
Whose father begged and screamed as he followed through the undertakers
        of blood-robotted streets of White City Jabavu
        Through Nip an' Two Beers accompanied by girls from
        Los-my-cherie drinking the blood of the loveless
        Through prisons of vengeance where the matjietas blom
He followed scraping his son's sperm dripping from gushing and
        torn wombs of Afrika Motherhood.
He followed, tired, with two great holes of poverty mocking him
        from the bottom of his shoes and found
His hope lay bleeding on the rubble of a slum clearance
At the funeral: the father wore black
                   the mother wore black
                   the priest wore black
                   the people wore black
They all cursed their blackness.
O victory put on your coat we are losing the battle to stay alive.

Motlase Mogotsi

Soul's Disparity

We came from faraway,
    from a land of darkness and continuous wars;
Where light seemed very strange to watch,
    the roads there were dangerous with dongas
        gaping at the sun.

When shall we see the sun again
    in this droning night resistant to sleep?
And caress the warm breeze
    from seas of fraternity and love?

We felt western belief
    embracing change in our sleep
We drank this to our fill
    and now we have our eyes glued on the moon!

O, how we sheltered our heads
    under roofs of civilisation . . .
And froze our hopes in regrets
    for having allowed poor souls to practise an
        alien life!

But every day, when civilisation enlightens our souls,
    we drag our feet in despair . . .

The Unforgettable Mistake

We headed for the mountains
Keeping our little fire to ourselves
Which for many years
Our forefathers kept burning
In their sacred huts.

Surprisingly, a stranger came
Bribed us into deserting
Our life-line,
which we did
Without a thought!

Behind the mountains
We helped erect a monument
To his previous victories
Which we did not know of.

Then, at the sound of the state drum
We embraced, singing for the day's fortunes
Proudly tramping at our achievements
Unaware of the little fire burning out behind;
The life ball of our lives!
So happy was the stranger
Who arrested us all
For our foolishness . . . !

David Moja-Mphuso

Old Homes

the sun showing the place every morning,
Where every reflection of our eyes
is attracted to our ancestors,
their deeds destined to become memorials of today.
If only we could, unashamed, place those cornerstones again
to be our stepping stones,
discipline carried from mother's knee,
learned there, the family
and all to be the sand of the same
home, with all the branches again
of the same heart.
Why not the body of the land forever
like the ruins of Zimbabwe,
why not my rooigrond living on
the spirits of our ancestors buried there?
While false beliefs like glue
hold our new homes together . . .

Nape á Motana

Village from the Portion of my Mind
(Abstract painting by Thami ka Mnyele)

A livid wind sweeps
  with monstrous brooms
Leaving 4 huts 4 cows
  donkeyleg skeleton, a shrub
and frail dew-ridden cobwebs.

Moody colours are torpid
  while entombed
Grey is more palpable
Cannibal rocks emerge
  as the soil is airborne
    to Chieftainess Moon.

The sap of beings floats
  like a creamcoat
Salty voices crawl
  like witchwhispers
Seashells domesticate mixed bones
  But the white-hearted sea
    sifts 4 fleshy faces
glued to the pale-blue firmament
without shedding a single spark.
Tantalizing mama
evokes and fans fire-in-eyes
Hungering faces cry:
'Mama, nyanga!
Mama, nyanya!'

But a cloud-chunk drizzles
and blazing hope fizzles.

Molahlehi wa Mmutle

Our Immortal Mother

My mother died a servant
She was buried a meid
A house meid she was
Like a dienskneg she lived
With all humanity removed

On a plank bed she slept
Supported by four Gokoks
Wrapped in a shoal of bags
Covered with rags from her Missies
Radiance of colour and design faded

She scrubbed the floors
Washed their underwear
Like a soulless brute she worked
She had no soul they said
Was she not born to suffer

She ate out of a broken plate
Drank from a cup without handle
Those were oorskiets and krummels
From her divine master's table
Were they not destined to be Masters?

My armsalige Moeder
Sy was te goed om te lewe
Te eerlik vir die wêreld
Mag die Almagtige haar seën
Haar trane, haar bloed lewe

Like a servant she was rewarded
With oud klere and huisraad
She had a Sunday off
To pray and thank their God
For their godheid and genade

They killed her
She died in solitude
Broken — broken to the bone
Without raising an eye to heaven
For the foreign God betrayed her

She lives on in her shrine
Her soul they could not destroy
She went to rest, a goddess,
Worshipped by those she loved
Immortalised by her children

Es'kia Mphahlele

Death

You want to know?
My mother died at 45
at 42 my brother followed.
You want to know?
She cleaned the houses of white folk,
and washed their bodily dirt
out of the baths.
One night a coma took her,
and he —
cancer hounded him two years
and rolled him in the dust.
You want to know?
My grandma left at 80,
she also washed her years away
and saw them flow
into the drain
with the white man's scum.
Many more from our tree have fallen —
known and unknown.

... and that white colossus
he was butchered by a man
they say is mad.

How often do I dream
my dearest dead stand across a river —
small and still I cannot traverse
to join them
and I try to call to them
and they wave and smile so distantly
receding beyond the water
that pulls me in
and spits me out into the dawn of the living.

... and he was butchered
like a buffalo
after overseeing many a negro's execution.

You want to know —
why do I say all this?
what have they to do with us
the ones across the water?
How should I know?
These past two decades
death has been circling closer

and beating the air about me
like a flight of vultures
in a cruel age
when instruments of torture
can be found with any fool and tyrant,
churchman, all alike,
all out to tame the heretic, they say.

. . . and they tell us
when the colossus fell
he did not even have a triple-worded
Roman chance

And so to kill a bug
they set a house on fire
to kill a fire
they flood a country
to save a country
drench the land in blood
to peg the frontiers of their colour madness
they'll herd us into ghettoes
jail us
kill us slowly
because we are the Attribute
that haunts their dreams
because *they* are the blazing neon lights
that will not let us be
because we are the children of their Sin
they'll try to erase the evidence
because their deeds are howling from a fog
beyond their reach.

. . . and we laughed and danced
when news came of the death of that colossus
— the death of a beast of prey.

What can we do with the ashes of a tyrant?
who will atone?
whose blood will pay for those of us who went
down under the tanks of fire?
And voices cried It's not enough,
a tyrant dead is not enough!
Vengeance is mine and yours and his,
says the testament of man
nailed to the boulder of pain.

. . . and they say the butcher's mad
who sank the knife into the tyrant's neck
while the honourable men
who rode his tanks of fire

looked on
as if they never heard of giants die
as they had lived,
and all about the frog who burst
when he pushed his energy
beyond the seams of his own belly.

What if I go as the unknown soldier
or attended by a buzzing fly?
what if my carcass were soaked in organ music,
or my ancestors had borne me home?
I hear already
echoes from a future time of voices
coming from a wounded bellowing multitude
cry Who will atone
Who will atone?

You want to know?—
because I nourish
a deadly life within
my madness shall have blood.

Somewhere

Somewhere a mother sobs
through bomb-shattered nights
hunger drains the blood of children.
Somewhere we eat the sputum of our pride
when we know nothing and we blunder.
Somewhere a woman sees her sick man
teeter on the edge of midnight
and turn his back to her and all forever.
Somewhere in the arena we lose our heads
amid the boos and jeers and whoops
along the sidelines.
Somewhere a mother waits
her man, her son
in chains of an oppressor
or waits for those who never come
and still endures we know not how.
And yet amid the smoking debris
of a fear-driven world
while man juggles with megaton eggs,
somewhere a woman gives the world an artist:
a child who sings and dances,
dreams and weaves a poem round the universe
plunging down the womb
to fire a cell
sinking down a borehole

to probe the spring of life
from where the earth will rise
to meet the sky.
Somewhere in ancient China, it is told,
a man made a song
out of the wailing of a dove
a song that moved all animals
to rise and kill the serpent
who ate the bird's young ones.
To know our sorrow
is to know our joy —
somewhere a mother will rejoice.

Fathers and Sons

Fifteen years ago
they dragged me out at dawn
blindfolded me and shot me,
      then -
eternity wrapped me up
in my dazzling blackness.

Now you see
I have returned with others —
not like Lazarus
jolted from his grave,
maybe even grousing
that they yanked him out of sleep
that he so badly needed;
not like Lazarus
rubbing off the particles of sleep
and wobbling up the hill
to wait upon
the edge of the cliff
for a second going.

I come with fury
raising cyclones with my feet
and I have come to stay
come another dawn of firing squads.
Tell me not of second comings
or love of God:
      I cannot feel it
      never have in all my terror-stricken years:
all I know
is that I'm 15 years of age
is that I feel the prison's cold and vermin
      crawling over me and nibbling on my heart
is that already I have seen the voltage
      in the fences of the law

is that I'm scared
because last night they buried many bodies
        in a big-big hole.
Tell my Mama that I'm scared
hear me tell you that I'm scared
of them with hairy arms and yellow fingers
        shooting out like sausages.

Tell her that they asked me who's my father
and I said to them he's dead
and one of them had bluestone eyes
and ears like he was going to fly
and now I hear my Mama's words about
a man they dragged outside at dawn
the sunset burning in his hooded eyes
and —
and now my heart is telling me —
that man with bluestone eyes
has *got* to have been there at dawn.

Daizer Mqhaba

Tshisa-Nyama

The very fact that it is isolated
From other shops proves the reality:
This is a Bantu Special Restaurant
Owned by all Italian team-mates.

The pap, you braai till it turns chocolate brown
The meat and the wors, you leave in the red oven
Till it resembles our customers' colour.
The binnegoeters, you leave half-raw, half-cooked.

The shop, you don't label the name.
The tables must be of hard steel, the chairs as well.
The plates must be of aluminium,
The spoons, big, round and rusty.

The advertisement must be fuming smoke
That is burning meat and pap.
Let a Bantu man call it Tshisa-nyama,
We don't mind the queries and all such.

The soup must be made from a cheap recipe,
The ingredients as costless as ever.
The sweets must be sticky, and also Dube-Dubes.
Cigarettes? mainly B.B., Lexington and Mboza.

When he orders he must be as audible as a motor horn.
Should he warble like a swallowing Bull,
Give him any item in front of you —
He'll not lodge even a single complaint.

Business manners — not applicable to him.
Just shout at him: 'Funani Bhizzah?'
He'll never wrinkle — 'Funa Pap en Steik!'
And then draw shekels from a dirty horseshoe-pouch.

Same, must be wrapped in an inky Newspaper
He must eat outside on the dusty stoep
Who does he think will clean for him
After finishing with all those remnants?

The suitable drinks served are usually:
Al Mageu, Hubbly-bubbly and Pint —
If he wants something decent, try next door!
We sell only Bantu appetising stuff here.

He must eat like a pig stuck in the mud,
His teeth must emphasize the echo of the
Battle with the whitish-pink coarse tongue.
He's mos never taught any table decency!

It is a restaurant solely for Bantus.
No other race has any business to interfere,
The food sold here is absolutely fire-smelling:
Sies! I'll never eat that kind of junk! Ga!

Tshisa Thixo safa Yindelelo!

Oupa Thando Mthimkulu

Nineteen Seventy-Six

Go nineteen seventy-six
We need you no more
Never come again
We ache inside.
Good friends we have
Lost.
Nineteen seventy-six
You stand accused
Of deaths
Imprisonments
Exiles
And detentions.
You lost the battle
You were not revolutionary
Enough
We do not boast about you
Year of fire, year of ash.

Mothobi Mutloatse

Mamellang
(or, Jumbled Thoughts)

There are
times,
bazalwana,
when men
I mean real he-men
who don't
indulge
in pure and ungodly
deeds
feel down at heart,
that their lives
are ill-spent
like the yearly rising rents,
and would rather offer
their earthly souls
to mother nature
than be devoured
painstakingly by other cannibalistic ogres
and demons —
bipeds, with sound-boxes to reason —
called, 'human beings',
the Almighty's creations,
and, paradoxically,
some booze and wallow in splendour
and as you prick their skins, what! —
out oozes red wine!
aha!
overlook the
exclamations—
and continuing—-while others
(the poor souls)
languish in squalor
'cause
many value
life so cheaply
(God have mercy)
and yet only a chosen few
deem it
so dearly.

Ngwana wa Azania

a proemdra for oral delivery

- The future of the black child, the recalcitrant Azanian child in South Africa, is as bright as night and this child, forever uprooted, shall grow into a big sitting duck for the uniformed gunslinger.
- From ages two to four he shall ponder over whiteness and its intrigue. From ages five to eight he shall prise open his jacket-like ears and eyes to the stark realisation of his proud skin of ebony. From ages nine to fifteen he shall harden into an aggressive victim of brainbashing and yet prevail. From ages sixteen to twenty-one he shall eventually graduate from a wavering township candle into a flickering life-prisoner of hate and revenge and hate in endless fury. This motherchild shall be crippled mentally and physically for experimental purposes by concerned quack statesmen parading as philanthropists.
- This motherchild shall be protected and educated free of state subsidy in an enterprising private business asylum by Mr Nobody. This motherchild shall mother the fatherless thousands and father boldly the motherless million pariahs. This nkgonochild shall recall seasons of greed and injustice to her war-triumphant and liberated Azachilds. This mkhuluchild shall pipesmoke in the peace and tranquillity of liberation, and this landchild of the earth shall never be carved up ravenously again and the free and the wild and the proud shall but live together in their original own unrestricted domain without fear of one another, and this waterchild shall gaily bear its load without a fuss like any other happy mother after many suns and moons of fruitlessness in diabolical inhumanity.
- This gamble-child of zwêpe shall spin coins with his own delicate life to win the spoils of struggle that is life itself. This child of despair shall shit in the kitchen; shit in the lounge, shit in the bedroom-cum-lounge-cum-kitchen; he shall shit himself dead; and shall shit everybody as well in solidarity and in his old-age shall dump his shit legacy for the benefit of his granny-childs: this very ngwana of redemptive suffering; this umtwana shall but revel in revealing off-beat, creative, original graffiti sugar-coated with sweet nothings like:
   re tlaa ba etsa power/re-lease Mandela/azikhwelwa at all costs/we shall not kneel down to white power/release Sisulu/jo' ma se moer/black power will be back tonight/release or charge all detainees/msunuwakho/down with booze/Mashinini is going to be back with a bang/to bloody hell with bantu education/don't shoot — we are not fighting/Azania eyethu/masende akho/ majority is coming soon/freedom does not walk it sprints/inkululeko ngoku!
- This child born in a never-ending war situation shall play marbles seasonably with TNTs and knife nearly everyone in sight in the neighbourhood for touch and feel with reality, this child of an insane and degenerated society shall know love of hatred and the eager teeth of specially-trained biting dogs and he will speak animatedly of love and rage under the influence of glue and resistance.
- This marathon child shall trudge barefooted, thousands of kilometres through icy and windy and stormy and rainy days and nights to and from rickety church-cum-stable-cum-classrooms with bloated tummy to strengthen him for urban work and toil in the goldmines, the diamond mines, the coal mines, the platinum mines, the uranium mines so that he should survive countless weekly rockfalls, pipe bursts, and traditional faction fights over a

meal of maiza that has been recommended for family planning.

- This child of raw indecision and experimentation shall sell newspapers from street corners and between fast moving cars for a dear living bread-winning instead of learning about life in free and compulsory school, and shall provide the capitalistic country with the cheapest form of slavery the labourglobe has ever known and the governor of the reserve bank shall reward him with a thanks-for-nothing-thanks-for-enriching-the-rich kick in the arse for having flattened inflation alone hands-down.

- This child of the tunnels shall occasionally sleep malunde for an on-the-spot research into the effects of legalised separation of families and he shall find his migrant long-lost father during a knife-duel in a men's hostel and his domestic mother shall he ultimately embrace passionately in a cul de sac in the kitchen in a gang-bang.

- This child of concrete shall record and computerise how the boss shouts and swears publicly at his heroically shy father-boy and how the madam arrogantly sends his mother-girl from pillar to bust. He shall photograph how the superior doctor addresses his unkempt mother in untailored talk as if mother-stupid had conceived a baboon-child.

- This observant child shall taste its first balanced meal in an i.c.u., and in the very intensive care unit shall he be revived to further life and misery and malnutrition in this immensely-wealthy land to loosen up the bones down to their perforated marrow.

- This child of the donga shall watch in jubilation and ecstasy and ire as its godforsaken, godgiven home called squatter camp is razed through its permission down to the ground by demolishing bulldozers lately referred to as front-enders.

- This child of nowhere shall of his own free will join the bandwagon and ravaza its own Botshabelo to lighten the merciless soil conservationists' burden for a place in the sun of uncertainty, he shall show absolute respect for his elders with a hard kierie blow across the grey head and shall be unanimously nominated for a nobel peace prize for his untold, numerous contributions to human science at a local mortuary.

- This child born into a callous and too individualistically-selfish society shall be considered sane until further notice by psychopaths masquerading as men of law. He shall be an unmatched hero with an undecided following, having paralysed parents and preachers alike with his frankness and willingness not only to whisper nor speak about wanting to be free but to bloody well move mountains to be free!

- This child of evictions shall sleep in toilets while its off-spring cross the borders for possible m.t.

- This child of rags to rags and more rags to riches school uniform tatters shall quench his thirst with dishwater in the suburbs and also with methylated spirits in the deadendstreet camps to communicate with the gods.

- This child shall breastfeed her first baby before her seventeenth birthday and be highly pleased with motherhood lacking essential fatherhood. This child of uneasiness shall trust nobody, believe in no one, even himself, except perhaps when he's sober. This ghettochild shall excel in the pipi-olympics with gold and bronze medals in raping grannies with every wayward erection and eviction from home resulting from ntate's chronic unemployment and inability to pay the hovel rent.

- This growing child of the kindergarten shall psychologically avoid a school uniform admired telegraphically by uniformed gunfighters of maintenance of chaos and supremacy. He shall smother moderation goodbye and throttle reason in one hell of a fell swoop, and the whole scheming world shall cheer him up to the winning post with its courage in the mud and its heart in its pink arse. This child of dissipation shall loiter in the shebeen in earnest search for its parents and shall be battered and abused to hell and gone by its roving parents when reunited in frustration in an alleyway.
- This child of bastardised society and bastard people-in-high-office and colour-obsession of paranoid of communism and humanism, shall break through and snap the chain of repression with its bare hands, and this child, with its rotten background and slightly bleak future shall however liberate this nuclear crazy world with Nkulunkulu's greatest gift to man: ubuntu.
- This lambschild shall remind the nation of the oft-remembered but never-used ISINTU:

Mangwana o tshwara thipa ka fa bogaleng.

Mandla Ndlazi

A Visit to Isandhlwana
July 15 1978

Wings of concern carried me
To the solemn monument
Where I bowed on my knee
Just a moment the other day
And spoke to my ancestors.

The gaping mountain craned
Over the memories
And silent graves
Of a British mistake.

My shudder pulsed from there
Reaching callous clouds that gather
To darken the counsel of peace

And I heard a bull bellow
As it pawed the dust
Shattering the thoughtful silence
Of rolling rock-strewn plains,
And a vulture flapped across
The film set readied to re-enact
A folly that's familiar.

Nthambeleni Phalanndwa

In this World, my Sister

I
It all started in the church
We looked each other in the eyes
Your devastating smile
Yes, it made me forget reality
My mind a radio
Playing two stations at a time
And I listened to both
The faint voice of the preacher
And the sweet loud voice
Conveyed by your smile.

The preacher continued to talk
While I sat there
Like a fly to be swallowed by a frog
So innocently in love
And people started to sing
While from another world
I heard them faintly from afar.

We became correspondents for a year
Me writing sweet letters to you
You writing sweeter ones in return
And we were happy and grateful
For that was friendship
But even so
Visit each other we could not
I had no money
And you had no time.

Correspondence continued
Until you had to ask
As I continued to write
Calling you darling sometimes
Without calling it a spade
Then I poured it all out
All I felt at the church
The first time we met
And in reply you said:
'The best evidence
of our love
Is not a long letter
Or something big
It is the little things
That we do day by day
that best say

I LOVE YOU.'
On that Saturday you came
where I used to dwell
All day long
We sat on the bricks
We caressed, kissed and cried

For it was sweet
With veins like copper conductors
In which flew electrons of love
Mouths serving as a switch
And the circuit was complete
Both benumbed
We sat there
And forgot
That we had no chair.
In the evening when I cooked
You sat on those bricks
Unconcerned,
Loving me.
After we had eaten
You congratulated me
On the delicious food I cooked
And it was night.
After reading you some poems
You asked for water
To wash your face and feet
I looked at your bare torso
And saw your pointed breasts so proud.

We got between the blankets
Two on the floor
And one on us
Again
You never complained.

For a month you went on leave
You neither wrote nor came
You later wrote to tell why
It was due to heavy rains
That left the people homeless and starving.

II
My dear J,
These things do happen in the lives of men
That sons and daughters
Are separated from their parents
Husbands separated from their wives
And during such times
We sit down
Balance our heads between our hands

Look into the skies
We see the future bleak.

We feel our legs go lame
Our hearts dead within our bodies
Fear-stricken people
Living in deadly fear of a knock on the door
For who knows
You may be next
To leave your next of kin.

But this, I will not discuss
Lest I bring down
The wrath of heaven and earth on my head
I leave it as a legend
For fathers to tell their children one day.

Only memories fill my mind now
I am empty of love
Hate is what I see
Written all over people's faces
Carving furrows that make them look like scarecrows.

The dead are dead my sister
We cannot ask them questions
The living must answer
They must tell us all we want to know
They must tell us now
For in this world my sister
No more
No more can I go on seeking
Justice, fairness and truth
These things do not exist.

I tried to walk
And stopped along the way
The signboard was dumb
I didn't know which road to take
I just stood and gazed
But the signboard did not tell
Only in my memories of the past
I saw a man playing an accordion in church.

But there in church
The congregation waited and hoped
But the priest did not come
And there at school
Students to write exams within a fortnight
With half of the syllabus still undone
Waited for their history teacher with hope
But the teacher did not come.

I want to suggest
That we go into the bushy mountains
And see if baboons are caged
Let's go to the seas
And see if fishes no longer swim
Perhaps we shall understand
That the change has come
Through the will of

                GOD
                        THE SON
                                AND THE HOLY GHOST

You gods of Africa
And you my father I do not blame you
But you never told me
That the sun rises and sets
That flowers bloom and wither
That this world grows thorny trees
That prick the feet
I have been burnt
I now dread the fire
My heart wails
It keeps on bleeding
The wounds are deep
Big gashes left there
By broken pieces of ...

At least
Beyond the distant horizon
The sun still shines
                        THERE
                        NOW
I want to go   THERE
                        NOW
Go quietly   THERE
                        NOW
Speak to nobody
Address the winds
Greet my friends the immortal boulders
Mortal beings can force you to hate
And hate and hate ...

But when you have an aim in life
It is like travelling in a tunnel
The darkness worries you not
The little light at the other end
Is comfort enough to kill your bitterness.

Right now
I bid you farewell my sister
People do meet and part
Children get born
Some die young . . . these are fortunate
But on the thoroughfare of life
Let's both go our separate ways
I want to toddle out of this limbo
Up until I cross the Limpopo
Alone.

Then I will start my march
Until I cross the River Congo
And if not dead with fatigue
I will reach Cameroon
To meet Mbella Sonne Dipoko
I want to meet him and ask
If he knows what they do in the veld.

Then I will continue my march
Until my destination is reached
And here
I want to talk to Cyprian Ekweni
Have lunch with Chinua Achebe
And I will ask them
If they know the veld
I want to tell them
That there
Baboons do eat mealies during the night
Then they will write
And the world shall know
What is happening in the veld
And on their advice
I will settle down
And learn at Ibadan.

No more turning back
I have seen enough of the veld
Where our lives are not our own.

Kriben Pillay

A Letter to Bandi*

This letter comes to you
empty of the things
I wanted to say
empty of the shock, the horror,
the pain of the day
framing only black marks
on a white page
framing only hopes
in a fearful age
this letter comes to you
with all my love
but
empty of the things
I wanted to say
framing only black marks
on a white page.

*This poem was written on the occasion of the detention of
Bandi Mvovo, who was detained on 11 September 1978.

Magoleng wa Selepe

My Name
Nomgqibelo Ncamisile Mnqhibisa

Look what they have done to my name . . .
the wonderful name of my great-great-grandmothers
Nomgqibelo Ncamisile Mnqhibisa

The burly bureaucrat was surprised
What he heard was music to his ears
'Wat is daai, sê nou weer?'
'I am from Chief Daluxolo Velayigodle of emaMpodweni
And my name is *Nomgqibelo Ncamisile Mnqhibisa.*'

Messia, help me!
My name is so simple
and yet so meaningful,
but to this man it is trash . . .

He gives me a name
Convenient enough to answer his whim:
I end up being
Maria . . .
I . . .
Nomgqibelo Ncamisile Mnqhibisa.

Eugene Skeef

We the Dancers

We the dancers
Greeted the sun
Sitting by the lowest step
Of the curtained house
We were the old nurse
For the faded child
See the way we felt
In the blueness of her eye
We will sit
Before the house was built
We will drink our tears
Before her eye could blink
When we will dance
We were free . . .

We the dancers
Came dead with the fetching flame
We were the fly
The fires feared
Yet took for our wings' release
We waited as the bars
Held in cell window-sills
For the off-beat
We will slip
Before the count was expected
When we will fly
The sun was borne in our pinion . . .

We the dancers
Awoke the bare earth
To yield to the tattoo
Our temper beat
The senile moth moulted
Beyond the strains of the nocturne
Our lowered foot
Quivered at the ordination
Of an apprenticed midwife
Far from the African wharf
Oblivious of its prophetic poise
Even the squeak
Of the lower deck
Could not shame the resonance
Of the sibilant silence
Of our bearing wave
The minor cadence of our song

Groaning aloft the Atlantic storm
As we dance to go
To become loose
In the flesh of the apple
We will skin too the serpent
Before the earth wore trees
Men we will move
The waters have 'brought forth
Abundantly the moving creatures
That have life . . .'

Farouk Stemmet

Custodian of our Spirit

oh Baobab
you stand firm
in the soil
in which you always stood
you stand firm
in the soil
in which you will always stand

your wrinkled bark testifies
to a memory
rich in times and events
long forgotten by man

you are not the rolling tide
you are not the changing cloud
you are neither the weeping willow
nor the departing ibis
you are not fallible man

you have never been colonised
you have always belonged
to the soil in which you stand

though your branches
may be chopped and pruned
you remain yourself
for your roots are secure
in the soil
which gave you birth

though your trunk is wide
and exposed to much
you can shield many

though the air about you may change
you will live forever

'Oh Africa seek your Spirit in me'

Essop Patel

On the Steps

in
the midnight hour
i heard
a sad song

in
the heat of the night
i heard
a dry groan

in the blistering dawn
i heard
a skull crack

on
the prison steps
i saw
a broken guitar
and
my brother's blood.

Barbed Wire Silence

Barbed wire silence
constricts me,
nothing moves
except
the sensuous realisation
of time
through the growing nostalgia.
The orange harvest
an indolent fulfillment,
the rustic scene
and the spangled seasons
an escapist wonderment.

Baby Thembisa

*'That Justice is a blind goddess
Is a thing to which we blacks are wise ...'*
                                        Langston Hughes

The charge sheet read:
                State v Baby Thembisa
One adult Bantu male of no fixed address, charged under
the Abuse of Dependence-producing Substances etcetera
Act No 41 of 1971, for being in possession of 20 dagga
cigarettes on Republic Day, 31st of May, 1971.

I entered the cement cold
underbelly of Jo'burg's
magistrates court,
for consultation
with my client,
the said Baby Thembisa,
regarding the aforementioned
allegation
made by the Drug Squad.

I saw my client naked,
sitting on the concrete floor
like a lotus flower,
reading CRIME & PUNISHMENT.
He said,
'Justice is a blind goddess
is a thing to which we blacks are wise...'

Houghton Party/Saturday Night Sunday Morning Poem

it's saturday night
let's have a party
in penny lane...

obla-di-obla-da-la-la-lah

good golly miss molly dancing with pretty flamingo
along comes mary carrying teddy bear
the brown eyed girl from spanish harlem
saying
sally go around the roses
if you can't find the loo
motor cycle irene in leather california dreaming
lady jane suggesting
let's spend the night together

obla-di-obla-da-la-la-lah

between bits & pieces feeling groovy
babylove with lucky lips
cooing
i can't get no satisfaction
between cheap wine & screw
everyone is unconcerned
with the subsiding sounds of soweto

da-da-dum-dum-du-um

sunday morning headlines:
everybody's been burned

da-dum-duuu-uuum

in the sound of silence
black suzanne placing
misty roses
on her brother's coffin...

They Came at Dawn

(for Omar)

Beyond
   the Carlton Centre
the sunbeams
   projecting
like warheads,
   they came
in uniform trucks,
   they came
rapping thunder
   on the door,
asking
   questions,
demanding
   answers.

They came at dawn
   they left at dusk
taking a poem
   written
on a bronze autumn leaf,
   written
in the shadow of bars,
   as evidence
for a banning order.

K. Zwide

Wooden Spoon

I carved a spoon from a rose-root
and, though thornless, its shape was strange,
conforming with the twisted nature
of the rose's journey into the earth.

Grandfather carved a straight spear
of a fine yellow wood;
melted ironstone with oxfat
and beat the blade on a rock,
and, blessing it with leaves and milk,
he whirled it into the air.
In response to gravity
it pierced his heart.

Now I eat with a crooked spoon
which I have dug from my master's garden
and it pierces my heart.

Christopher van Wyk

Metamorphosis

Hardly out of a napkin,
into the sixties
Sharpeville
scattered around my father
in newsprint
and me
fidgetting around his work-worn body
asking questions at his shaking head.

That memory has never yellowed
with age.

Now, after June 16
puberty attacks suddenly.
I wriggle bewildered in fertile hair.
I nod my head.
Now I understand.

Injustice

Me, I cry easily if you're hurt
and I would've carried the crosses
of both the murderer
and the thief
if they'd've let me
and I'd've lived then.

I grasp helplessly at cigarettes
during riots
and burn my fingers
hoping.

My nose has never sniffed teargas
but I weep all the same
and my heart hurts
aching from buckshot.

My dreams these days are policed
by a million eyes
that baton-charge my sleep
and frog-march me into a
shaken morning.

I can't get used to injustice.
I can't smile no matter what.

I'll never get used to nightmares
but often I dream of freedom.

About Graffiti

Graffiti is the writing on the wall
the writing on the wall as at Western
Heroes die young

In Noordgesig you'll see graffiti
Why Lord can't we live together?

Smeared on a wall in Eldorado Park
Love is?

In an alley somewhere
Sex is unlimited

Graffiti is painted on a wall
in District Six
Welcome to Fairyland

Graffiti can move too
Graffiti worms out of noses
of slum kids

Graffiti scrawls in piss
calls itself V.D.
clogs in priapic places-hurts

Bob Marley shouts reggae
from township cafés
'A hungry stomach
is a hungry man
Graffiti'

Graffiti is a dirty child
who scratches for sweets
and himself
in rubbish dumps

Graffiti is the gang
the gang who burnt a nice-time cherrie
and left her behind the shops
for dogs to eat off her left leg

Graffiti is children playing
around broken live wires from lampposts
and the Electricity Department fixing it
after somebody has burnt to death

has been shocked through the conduits
of his slum ignorance

When one black child tells another
'Ek sal jou klap
dan cross ek die border'
it's graffiti

and

When another child says
'I don't like Vorstra and Kruga
because they want us
to speak Afrikaans'

Graffiti screams from a sonorous woman
as the hymens of her sanity rupture
suddenly
in a night

Graffiti shouts from the lips of a township
Kyk voor jou die Welfare sal agte jou kyk

Graffiti calls Soweto Sovieto

Graffiti is a scar on a face

The mine dump is graffiti

A cockroach is graffiti

Candle grease is graffiti

A rabid dog is graffiti

Adrenalin and blood in the township,
that's graffiti

Soon graffiti will break loose
into an ugly plethora
drift into Jo'burg
soil share certificates
deface billboards
dishonour cheques
drown managers, clerks, executives

Soon graffiti will wade into Jo'burg
unhampered by the tourniquet of influx control

Me and the Rain

Tonight it rains.
Hitting hard against the rooftops.
Thundering at the windowpanes.
All night through, aggressively
it smashes down upon the earth.
The dogs whimper.
But it rains until it stops.
Pula! Pula! Pula!

Like a catharsis it rains,
Emptying the bellies of the sky.
The September night flows with fright.
I can barely hear myself talk.
I listen instead.
The rain gushes into yards, streets, dongas,
like menses,
spilling forth the stalled emotions of the dry season.
I listen to the rain.
Pula! Pula! Pula!

It rains throughout the night
and people sleep.
But I don't. I hear a rooftop
unclasp itself from a flat and
swing down onto the ground.
And the radio says it's an act of God.
And the insurance company says it's
a natural catastrophe.
And the council say it's not their fault.
And the tenants say it's a sin.
Still it rains.
Pula! Pula! Pula!

I sit in a dry corner at home.
I scratch dandruff and sip coffee.
I think of Duma and Don.
Of Dukuza and Caplan and Fhazel.
I think of Themba and of tomorrow
and I listen to the rain
and my heartbeat;
Boom! Boom! Boom!

The rain is powerful;
it opens graves,
it rains on the Island,
it crawls under cell walls,
it remembers bodies forgotten in holes,

brings them floating into courtrooms:
the habeas corpus.

The rain can coax a flower
out of loam, out of rock.
The rain can uproot euphoria.
The rain can gut consciences.
The rain inspires me.
Pula! Pula! Pula!

Beware of White Ladies when Spring is Here

Beware of white ladies
in chemise dresses
and pretty sandals
that show their toes.
Beware of these ladies
when spring is here.
They have strange habits
of infesting our townships
with seeds of:
geraniums pansies poppies carnations
They plant their seeds in our eroded slums
cultivating charity in our eroded hearts
making our slums look like floral Utopias.
Beware!
Beware of seeds and plants.
They take up your oxygen
and they take up your time
and let you wait for blossoms
and let you pray for rain
and you forget about equality
and blooming liberation
and that you too deserve chemise dresses
and pretty sandals that show your toes.
Beware of white ladies
when spring is here
for they want to make of you
a xerophyte.

Confession

i would
have brought
you
mulberries
but
they threatened
to explode
their mauve
corpuscles
all over
my
best shirt
so
i ate them

Catharsis

Sometimes during long silences
after emotional conversation
about the tenses in our lives
you suddenly lift your head from lifelines
and say:

There were times, Chris
when I wished I was the only child
Then there would've been enough food
to go around.

God how my friend can say things
we all felt at times
but rather left unsaid.

A Riot Policeman

The sun has gone down
with the last doused flame.
Tonight's last bullet
has singed the day's last victim
an hour ago.
It is time to go home.

The hippo crawls
in a desultory air of triumph
through, around fluttering
shirts and shoes full of death.
Teargas is simmering.

Tears have been dried by heat
or cooled by death.
Buckshot fills the space
between the maimed and the mourners.
It is time to go home.

A black man surrenders
a stolen bottle of brandy
scurries away with his life
in his hands.
The policeman rests the oasis
on his lips
wipes his mouth on a camouflaged
cuff.
It is time to go home.

Tonight he'll shed his uniform.
Put on his pyjamas.
Play with his children.
Make love to his wife.
Tomorrow is pay-day.
But it is time to go home now,
It is time to go home.

Candle

(for Caplan)

Read brother read.
  The wax is melting fast
  The shadows become obdurate
  and mock pantomimes of you
  laughing through crude cement
  in silent stage whispers.

Read brother read,
  though the wax lies heaped
  in the saucer
  and the silhouettes of gloom
  grow longer.

Read brother read.
  Only the wick shines red now.
  But it is not yet dark.
  Remember brother,
  it is not yet dark.

Zimbabwe

Henry Pote

To my Elders

Old enough am I through the span of years,
Yet neither tribal elder or settler my opinion hears.
My stand to the one is strange and preposterous
And to the other rampant, immature, boisterous.
Oft-times have I envied my forefathers' ignorance
When cattle, wives and grain meant abundance
With books, machines and ideologies of no consequence.
Man's destiny lay in Midzimu's indulgence.
My knowledge is impotent power gone sour.
The old and the new in me shall yet find,
In hope, in equal and blended
Measure, both inheritances; if not bemoan your distrust.
Condemn yourselves in me and die, as you entrust
To me what you denied me when you lived!

                                        (1966)

Godfrey Dzvairo

Follow my Mind
(On a fellow comrade's third anniversary in prison,
October 1969)

The old house at the corner
Grown familiar in seventeen life-filled years
Now seemed so strange.
They still loved you, you knew,
And the family wounds would soon heal over;
But you no longer belonged there.
Though you felt you knew the reasons
Words failed your desire to make a point
And now you sought your volume in action.
The east beyond Stoddart and Ardbennie* beckoned,
To the man in you that had taken root
Amongst the Julies and Annas of your priorities
And won.
You had grown
And this decision was the first of many
To matter more than films, festivals and fun;
The bigger family, Zimbabwe, needed you
And you gave yourself
With that quiet, almost secret farewell
On an indifferent Saturday morning,
Something I hope you do not regret
After three years of disillusionment
And a raw taste of life.

*Sections in the suburb of Harare

206

Eddison Zvobgo

My Companion and Friend:
The Bare Brick in my Prison Cell

The surface shines
Causing my eyes to flee
To the edges
Where the dull grey mortar
Mounts the brick
Marrying it to its neighbours.
But as I gaze
At this brick over seven years
Lying in my cage
Which measures four strides by three
An entire universe has sprung
All over its burnt-out terrain.

Slowly, the erstwhile smoothed
Face blossomed with islets
Ravines and dongas:
Here a Kariba, there a volcano
And then a Grand Canyon
Running westward Maluti Mountains.
No gales of wind blow
And no birds sing.
I have yet to discern cities
And highways, nor do I see
Lush green fields of maize and wheat.

We have become friends
Over the long years;
Both of us are deportees
From our homes and friends;
Both of us long to return from death
To the councils of our peers.
Does nobody care to remember
That perhaps these caked grains
Have fed some plant which gave forth

Grain or fruit for man?
Is this banishment to these wedges
Through form and fire deserved?

I have counted thousands
Of hungry granules on its face
Which cry for water
And hoe, hoping that they, too,
Might be fulfilled,
As I long to be free and fulfilled.

Next year, as I look
At the brick much more closely,
I shall be able to travel
On its terrain to the Louvre
In Paris and perhaps even go down
To the Riviera before I die.

Perhaps those sullen edges
May soon become the very
Outerspace that still remains
To be charted by modern
Technology and astronautics,
And I, share glory with Armstrong.

This brick insulates me
From myself, rendering me
As cold as salad.
I bear no grudge against it;
All I seek is a sworn treaty
Between us, so that when its purposes
And mine are done, it may
Cover my bones and consummate
Our seven years romance.

Paul Chidyausiku

Grandpa

They say they are healthier than me
Though they can't walk to the end of a mile;
At their age I walked forty at night
To wage a battle at dawn.

They think they are healthier than me:
If their socks get wet they catch a cold;
When my sockless feet got wet, I never sneezed —
But they still think they are healthier than me.

On a soft mattress over a spring bed,
They still have to take a sleeping-pill:
But I, with reeds cutting into my ribs,
My head resting on a piece of wood,
I sleep like a babe and snore.

They blow their noses and pocket the stuff —
That's hygienic so they tell me:
I blow my nose into the fire,
But they say that is barbaric.

If a dear one dies I weep without shame;
If someone jokes I laugh with all my heart.
They stifle a tear as if to cry was something wrong,
But they also stifle a laugh,
As if to laugh was something wrong, too.
No wonder they need psychiatrists!

They think they have more power of will than me.
Our women were scarcely covered in days of yore,
But adultery was a thing unknown:
Today they go wild on seeing a slip on a hanger!

When I have more than one wife
They tell me that hell is my destination,
But when they have one and countless mistresses,
They pride themselves on cheating the world!

No, let them learn to be honest with themselves first
Before they persuade me to change my ways,
Says my grandfather, the proud old man.

Musaemura Zimunya

No Songs

No songs of cicadas
Only a sighing silence
where once
as I walked below the yellow leaves
of fresh foliage
a spray of urine
moistened my face
and a shrill symphony
waned into my ears.

We have no ancestors
no shrine to pester with our prayers
no sacred cave where to drum our drums
and no *svikiro* to evoke the gods of rain
so we live on
without rain, without harvest.

No whistle of a bird
no flutter nor flap
amid the brown fingers of trees
without leaves
when spring's lushness
should be wiping my tired eyes
and dipping gleams of sunshine
into the young leaves.

Where shall we find the way back?
opaque darkness guards our exit
we have groped and groped until
our eyes were almost blind
it's hard to rediscover.

So we live outside the burning flames of our thirst
we live the lives of locust-hunting rooks,
but even then where are the rooks
for I have neither heard a caw
nor seen a black patch in the sky
the day we shall know the way back
to the caves of the ancestors,
the lion tongue of death will be licking
the last gush of blood from our souls.

(1972)

Efulamachina (Flying Machine)

An old man
toddled in his field
his mind full of his hunger
full of fears of his precious seeds:
sons, and multiplying grandchildren.
Always thinking:
he had seen the ends of the cool first rains,
the end of zhisha!*
of exploding green and milky cobs by the fireside
of harvests and festivals of millet beer
(weevils are beating drum skins under hovels)
he could reduce time
and count the years on his five fingers
everything else is coming to an end
people can still hold on, but not long
his thin self could think no more too.

Suddenly
it was thundering
and roaring everywhere
sand was vibrating
under the skin of the feet.

Slowly, surprised
like a semi-colon,
a bow-like hoe-handle
or like a spent nurau** of the hunter
smoky twiggy spectacles hidden
in the deep sockets of the eye
one hand on the walking stick
another grasping the back
like that of the alert locust

he stopped
and mantis-like
slowly turned his head
uttered a soft laughter
a scrappy 'kee-kee-kee'
from his toothless infant mouth
his eyes fixed on a black trail of smoke
turning into clouds
in the hazy blue sky
pulled a fine long whistle
to fill his heart with this wonder
and in half empty voice
said 'Efulamachina',
following the trail of smoke
with his squinting eyes
and an innocent gumful smile

until the black dot sunk behind the horizon,
'These men of the white skin,
even puffing into the face of God,
I swear through Chaminuka,***
they will finish us all off.'

*   Luxuriant
**   Trap
***   The Shona legendary hero who probably was warrior,
        magician, wiseman and many other things. Another
        explanation is that this figure was possibly a priest of
        the Mwari Cult.

Roads

We who could not grow feathers
upon this flesh of ours
who could not turn arms into wings
who sought to violate bounds
imposed upon our genius
found flight in steel things
jaguaring on the road.
The bird's flight is liberal
touches all buoyant possibilities of joy

the wind and the blue can offer
flight is in the blood and shaft:
freedom is not narrowed to
twenty-two-foot cobbled tar-strips
no deadly hazard ahead
no blind rises and sharp turns
no slip of the wing

(The bee machine drones)
black Icarus
whisky bottle in mouth
like a saxophone
cheeks full-blown
a woman caresses your pot-belly
like a hopeful python
(the lion-spirited engine roars)
friends in the back seat laugh
until faces turn into skeletons with joy
(machine sounds like a crescendo of pain)

A sharp dive
a plunge into the tar
this species cannot pirouette
without disaster
too much fury in the behind
too much steel and heat

212

then the lightning crash
and bodies cannoned out

And here, brother,
witness it:
a red-cliffed rift into the occiput
grey over blood flowing on the tar
a whole minced arm from
shoulder to fingernails
it could be days old
but absence of ants
tells you of its recence —
this dead distortion,
so different from life.

Suddenly, this human flesh isn't steel
even steel itself has burnt to ash
this skin and blood are not rock
knees up in the air
mock the drunkard
who lies generally and snores
and behold, brother,
the spread-eagled hands.
His eyes are closed.

Chimpanzee

Here you are
all wrinkles
and distant rheumy eyes

a photographer
captured you
shaggy chimp
dishevelled hair
squatty nose
above haphazard lips —
almost abandoned recesses

Someone had forgotten
to put the ears on
so hurriedly stuck on
the head rebels

Round glassy eyes
little pearls
in a matted jungle of wrinkles
unwinking, tired
downcast but full of distances:

branches of trees creeping in
chaotic harmony,
full of friends, birds,
animals of the wild
places seen and unseen
hunting grounds, mating,
and freedom!
smell of the earth and jungle

I can feel
the silent violence
boiling through that head
the pulse of irritable silence
the illusion that snapped
the meshed electric bars
and freed your soul everyday

But what is illusion?
What becomes of soul
when human hands
have built iron frontiers
and locked you up
teasing and laughing in fascination
while you thumped the fence
with burning impatience
and killing frustration
you nearly pulverised
a tourist's fingers one day.

White Padre*

You
whose smile is stained with rust of smoke
whose voice is a rotting breath of alcohol
(wardens probably washed your conscience off
with slow, detergent tots of gin
in the midst of anti-black humour)

Christ's imitator,
you freakish fan
you couldn't protest against Pilate
now where is your salvation?

Padre!
who knew black men
as potential converts
or a lot of impossible pagans
or thieves, thugs, rebels . . . .

214

You,
who knew not who made your roads
who knew not who toiled to dig coal
to make the all-weather tarred roads
who knew not us
why we threw the stones
and sent sharp glass tinkling into the faces**
of puzzled old clerks in those offices
who did not know how any lips
pronounced our prison sentences

You! You!
Preaching repentance.

* A prison chaplain who visited Zimunya and his mates
  while he was in prison.
** A reference to the 1975 University of Rhodesia student
  riots.

The Reason

(To Joy Lowe)*

In my letter
I feared the loss of love
inside my frame.
Apologies that it shocked you
I was only being frank.
Everyday you see all these men —
prisoners —
misery playing a dead show
in their countenances
laughing unconscious of
the negativeness their voices betray;
some of them too innocent to kill a louse
too old to know whether they are dead
or alive
the backs of these old men bled
perhaps they gave food to guerilla fighters
I was shown one back: an incomprehensible
tattoo of sjambok tracks showing pink
and this man will be here for five years
a grandad from the backwoods,
he knows not what Rhodesia is,
what Zimbabwe is or what this war is all about!
conscience lambasts you
like a gust of the August wind
disappears like a wisp of cigar smoke
questions unanswered block your thinking
frustration fumes and fumes

Now where is the room
for love?

*   A South African missionary who, with her husband,
    worked for years at Chikore Mission (Eastern
    Highlands) before being deported by the Rhodesian
    Front government. The Lowes are close friends of
    the poet.

After the Massacre

There was a row in the pub,
and, frankly speaking, the English landlord
was, to say the least, quite shaken.

But then we were customers,
exiles haunting every green place,
and so there was no bouncer in evidence
to pick up the pieces.

We castrated the regime,
we prophesied doom for the puppets,
we praised the work of the peasants,
managed to smash the capitalists,
and with a gulp the size and noise of a cataract
we cried, 'A luta continua!'*

Somewhere the CIA and BOSS got a roasting
and a guerilla leader was picked up
in the same bed as Lonrho,
and a hell of a rage ensued,
enough to demonstrate that
we have more righteousness than Livingstone had rated us with.
And, once more, 'A luta continua.'

The pilgrims from Denda
proclaimed themselves the future leaders
because no one could deny they had suffered the most
who would deny that they had fought the most
who would deny that they were the most educated.
and in a most accomplished stroke of genius
every tribe and clan was given the Anglo-Saxon equivalent —
Welsh, English, Scottish, Irish —
and our pyrrhic nature was complete.

The following morning
we considered the post mortem positive:
hadn't we talked about the wounds of the people,

hadn't you talked about their sore backs,
hadn't I talked about their deaths for our freedom,
I did mention their burning huts and that typhoid, didn't I?

Brother, well brother,
even with a hangover negotiating the head
like a goggelmander what we did not talk about
comes bleeding through the heat like a deep gangrene.

* Portuguese: the struggle continues

Rooster

What now, Rooster, Rooster,
now that there is no chicken-mother
to throw your wing-spread laughter around
and blow up dust in the run in the sun?

Rooster, Rooster,
you and I confront the acid side of life and things,
so, what, now, what indeed
now that the umbrella roof-top is no more —
fire once teased snarled all the way to ash —
where once your neck-stretched seizure of time
gave yellow dawn the form of sound?

In the village curfews have usurped your task
like plunder, and woe! the shadows astray.
Hunger and gangrene and disease and the smell
of burnt corpses and things
attest to the latest human appetite.

But nature has always provided us with abandon
as caves are home once again —
a century after Mzilikazi.

So stand on one leg on the mountain of Chitungwiza,
erect and cloud-high on the boulder's fontanelle
suspicious even of the sun with your eagle-searching eye
as true as the Zimbabwe bird,
herald at the edge of time, Rooster, Rooster,
awaken thunder with your wings
throw your eyes to the sky
and seizing the anguished moment in a throat
echo the overdue Hope
until Vhumba and Matopo answer:
else what dawn would you let us hear you announce?
                                              (1977)

Julius Chingono

To You Father

Father you have given them
Too much
Too much
They are buying spears
Arrows and bows

You have given them
Too much
Too much
They are trying your table
Your bed

Harken they are buying
Other gods!

Thank Thee Mother

I thank thee mother
Your back I wet
when I leaked
like a broken gourd,
your breast I sought
like a blind bat,
on your back
I swung like a little vagabond,
but you said
'It's my vagabond.'

Big Boys Don't Cry

That woman
In an oversize dress
That woman
The shadow of whose breats
Lingers in my mind
Lulled me then:
Big boys don't cry.

A small boy then:
Sure they don't cry
But sweat and sigh
For they have seen
More than one grass fire,

They have been stung
By more than one bee.

That woman
 Whose breasts are smaller
Than oversize watermelons
Taught me to die
Like a sheep.

Shimmer Chinodya

Recollection

I remember this wood only too well.
I remember these crouching thorn trees (— it seems
they've hardly grown ever since I last saw them —)
And these criss-crossing bush paths
Bordering a coarse crop of grass yellowed
With the dust stirred up
By swishing feet of children, and
The wind of course.
I remember too, the chirping of the timid little birds.

I remember how we used to run barefoot
Under these thorn trees.
Three brothers with feet full of thorns —
Bird-shooting we were, with rough-made little catapults
That exploded into our own faces.
And pockets full of jingling stones picked up somewhere.
Between us we shot down one bird in a year.

I remember the big sign that said
Something about people not being allowed in —
And we, heedless, half-ignorant prowlers
Made the wood our hunting-ground
And birds and bitter little berries our prey.

I remember it only too well . . .
I remember even more now, how young we were then
And how this scrub bush
Growing patched and ungreen — a short walk
From the township's street of grim houses
Satisfied our boyish dreams.

Kizito Muchemwa

Tourists

They came into the wilderness clichés in suitcases
Talismans they cherished as shields against this poisonous madness
Lurking in the dark aggressive landscape of alienness.
Looking for recognition of this my dear land
They saw no familiar hills and heard no familiar songs.
Holding onto their fetishes they defy time and distance
Send lines across oceans to tap the energies
A faceless past economically nourishes wilting roots
Dying on the rocky exposures of understanding through fear.

They surround themselves with jacarandas and pines,
Build concrete walls around their homes,
I hope next time they will import snow, change
The seasons to humour their eccentric whims.

Already other trinkets hoot their mockery of our lives
Proclaiming the raucous assertiveness of their makers
But this land, this; the spirits dwelling in it
Will not yield to such casual intimidation
Neither will it give out its rich sad secrets
To half-hearted tokens of transparent love.

Richard Mhonyera

Rhodes

A perpetual sinewy military strut
whose feet know not the ground
it stands on.

The eyes pierce through glass and brick of building
and what have you, to fix on
a point on the horizon.

The cars whizz by, casual, day after day;
on slower days, a passing look at the road-side curiosity
that has not the colour of men, with either touristic fascination,
or embarrassment,
or secret impotent denunciation.

Hence the wreaths of death would-be Rhodeses
garland him with, annually.

Samuel Chimsoro

Basket and Stones

(A Zimbabwean Spiritual)

There is life in a basket
For a baby lay safely in one
And found refuge among the reeds,
Found shelter and security
In a girl's infatuation.

There is life on a shoulder,
For the Rozvi and Changamires
Carried stones to a hill,
And built there a name
In which they found a home.

Tell men and women of the black strain,
Tell them the Lord says, 'get each a basket.'
Say, 'God commands you to join the racket
Of bringing stones, in sunshine or rain.'

You have no baskets at all,
You have no life in your baskets,
You have no life on your shoulders,
And you hope to build a bridge
Across the sea of injustices?

Listen to the Lord who is saying,
'Take pride in secrecy and responsibility.
Stand straight and progressive
Make stagnation your limit
Never fall into retrogression.' So

Tell men and women of the black strain,
Tell them the Lord says, 'get each a basket.'
Say, 'God commands you to join the racket
Of bringing stones, in sunshine or rain.'

There is life in a basket in the river.
Please get it to the pharaoh's daughter.
There is life on your strained shoulders
To be taken to your own home in your own name.

The Curfew Breakers

to walk in the sun
hoe in hand,
to dig drains
and engrave sorrow
on anthills
is for the love of life.

to sweep the streets
and fence the gates
to keep next-of-kin informed that
the right of admission
into the sun
is reserved
is for the love of life.

to turn to moonlight
for reflections of warmth,
to dance to drums
barefooted
and sanctify the earth
as the dust of ancestors
is freed from the earth
is for the love of life.

to sleep
on the skeletons of fallen stars
and dream that
the right of admission
into the darkness
is reversed
is for the love of life.

to wake up in the morning
as an object of dispute
and die in the evening
as a curfew breaker
is also for love of life.

The Change

What used to be
A missionary's poker
Is now a sceptre
Leaning against a sooted chimney.
The soft white wood
Has all burnt.
Its reluctant warmth is refuse
Diffused into the earth;
The grey covering ashy trash
Wanting to be blown.
What used to be
A gregarious row of chairs
Docks and electric seats
Is now a row of stone
Round an outdoor fire place
Loaded with 'mutsatsati' logs.
The heat of riots is gone
The heart of sermons is gone.
Speeches were concluded
Now speakers are redundant.
What used to be
So white is now all
In the museum of memory
While black hands dip
Lumps of their constitution
In the same soup bowl.

I Love

I love the silent majority
That rise earlier than the sun
To a breakfast of expectations.

I love the silent majority
Whose bread-eaters raise their eyes
To sensitise the bread-winners' backs
To their nudging anxieties.

I love the silent majority
For whom givers maximise
Fringe benefits with a whip
To sensitise the receivers' backs
To the costs of classes and races.

I love the silent majority
That for a week, a month, a century
Welcomes the empty-handed householder

Who nurtures them on hope
For their strength to sleep.

I love the curfew breakers
Who offer morsels of prayers,
Whispering loving complaints
For which they rest in peace
Beneath the feet of a sick society
That turns to snores
The snorts of nestlings
Mourning their deported householders.

I love the silent majority
That will rise earlier than the sun.

Pathisa Nyathi

Till Silence be Broken

Restless
Rich in ideas
Political dispensation
Social evils

Ideas
Only that?
No outlet?
Incommunicable?
Remain camouflaged
Glossed over
Never in black and white
White influencing black

Prose
Lets the cat out of the bag
Clear
Straight talk
Sells black to white
Black avoid white detection
Accusations otherwise your
Imprisonment sure next step
Hide black
Hide till silence be broken

Literary tools yours
Iron your formidable weapon
Verse your only sanctuary
Ambiguity
Imagery
Exploit fully
Remember Mark Antony
In his like incite

Write poets
Pass the message
Select intended victims
Conceal to all and sundry
Fool never to be apprehensive
In foolery be overtaken

Ideas
Abstract
Mothproof
Safe in carven

Controlled trickles
Along paths
Most safe
Most effective
Strike hard
But softly
Till silence be broken
Break the silence
Divorce ideas from mouth
Ideas strange to pen and paper
Verse your haven
Give expression to carven

Zimbabwe in verse
Wishes
Longings
All subtly put
Poets
Invisible revolutionaries
Motives well intentioned
Well put
Hidden
To oppressor
Till silence be broken
The revolution
In deep fathoms of verse
Undetected remain
Cultivated
Breaking the silence.

Chirwa P.Chipeya

Change

the clouds
losing the
lustre of
clarity
the sky
saturated
with imminent
tears
there's neither
breeze nor wind
to deceive
the vision
that the season
belongs
to the peasants

Today the War has Ended

Today
the war
has ended
the people sing
freedom has arrived
the people are singing
songs
of joy or
songs for the dead
                    (1980)

Charles Mungoshi

Burning Log

i am
a burning log
my history being reduced
to ashes
what i remember
of yesterday
is the ashy taste
of defeat
my hope
for tomorrow
is the fire.

If You Don't Stay Bitter and Angry
for too Long

If you don't stay bitter
and angry for too long
you might finally salvage
something useful
from the old country.

A lazy half-asleep summer afternoon
(for instance) with the whoof-whoof
of grazing cattle in your ears:
tails swishing, flicking flies away
or the smell of newly-turned soil
with birds hopping about
in the wake of a plough
in search of worms.

Or the pained look of your father.
The look that took you all these years
and lots of places to understand.

The bantering tone you took
with your grandmothers, and their old laugh
that said: 'nothing matters but death'.

If you don't stay bitter
and angry for too long
and have the courage
to go back:
you will discover that the autumn smoke
writes different

more hopeful messages
in the high skies
of the old country.

Mwari Komborerai Zimbabwe

('All Those Who Suffered for Zimbabwe')

First cockcrow; the rusty chains snap drop
The moth-eaten yoke crumbles into powdery dust
We break into the song denied us these ninety long years.

Go down on your knees, Brother: grab a clod of this earth
Do you feel the warmth in it?
Do you smell the hot blood
That glues its grains together?
Do you recognise it, Sister?
Yes. Let your tears cleanse and absolve you, my people.
You have refused to apologise or regret for living.

Jump into the new day, Sister,
Bathe yourself in the new dawn
Let the light annoint your wounds
Fly into the new wind, Brother,
Do you feel its freedomsong in your limbs?

Take this day, people of Zimbabwe, take this earth
Knead them and forge a new hopeful song that is all your own
A song that will echo through all generations to come
But a song that also remembers the mistakes
And the long bloody road through ninety years of dark despair and exile
When you sighed for a home yet a fire burned on your hearth.

Remember how it was —
To stand on firm earth
— And yet know your feet are in quicksand
to hold a calabash of spring water
— And know it'll be spilt before you take a sip
To clutch a morsel of *sadza*
— And have it snatched before you take a bite

Weave all this, weave it into the new song

Do not forget them who yearned so long for this song
Whose limbs now adorn open fields and furnish shallow graves
Bleached to their essentials by termites, sun, wind and rain
Forget not in your songs those who wanted to sing this song
Whose throats now are choked with mud, sand and silt
And remember them all, all of them

Who have brought back this song
To be heard once more in the land of your birth
In your time

Vanasekuru nanambuya —
Vose vakatambudzikira Zimbabwe —
Only you who have been thirsty
Can tell us what a drop of water is
Only you who have been hungry
Can tell us what a grain of *rukweza* means
Only you who have been bruised, blistered and burned
Can tell us about the evils of fire
You, whose souls have been honed and keened
Into the finest and sharpest feelers
Can tell us of the pain that is the birth
Of your children's inheritance: Zimbabwe!

Take this earth, then, Brother; feel its promise in your hand
(The same hand, Brother, that can spill blood, can shape life)
Do not clench your fist, Sister
Open your hand, you also, once-enemy-now-friend
Scatter this earth to the farthest corners of this land
— A tribute to the many who loved it and fell on it
Brew *doro rechenura*, my people, to bring them back home
For the dead live in the living
And the living are the seed of the dead
And the earth which abides forever
Gives sustenance to all
Who would live in the spirit of the land.

Mwari komborerai Zimbabwe

Canaan Banana

Liberating Love

Though I preach the sacred value of human life,
if I sit on my hands and watch the oppression of my people,
I am a hypocrite.

Though I approve of the goals of human liberation
and profess love for freedom,
if I do not act on this love it is worthless.

Though I think I can tell which way the wind is blowing,
if I let the moment to act pass me by,
I betray the imperative to love.

The people have suffered long; charity serves barely
to keep them alive. But charity by itself defuses
the will of the people to act.

Love is not defined from a book or a tradition —
it does not rest in its own abstract goodness;
it is shaped by the concrete needs of the people.

True love abhors evil; it rejoices in the struggle for the good.
On the path to triumph love can bear all things, hope all things;
it will not surrender.

Our need for justice and human dignity is as dear as life itself:
if there are political slogans they shall fade away;
if there are exploitative economic systems
they shall crumble and be changed.

For mankind cannot live by slogans alone.

Man's right to freedom and dignity is a gift from God,
thus when people together demand liberation,
that which oppresses shall give way.

For before I knew what it meant to have dignity,
I would neither see clearly nor love freely.
But when I began to struggle
I discovered the true meaning of Love.

When we were slaves, we spoke as slaves, we understood as slaves,
we thought as slaves;
but as we become free,
we cast off the chains of servitude.

So Faith, Love and Hope must abide: these three;
but without freedom and dignity
they remain hollow shadows.
(1980)

Angola & Mozambique

Noemia de Sousa

If You Want to Know Me

If you want to know me
examine with careful eyes
this bit of black wood
which some unknown Makonde brother
cut and carved
with his inspired hands
in the distant lands of the North.

This is what I am
empty sockets despairing of possessing life
a mouth torn open in an anguished wound
huge hands outspread
and raised in imprecation and in threat
a body tattooed with wounds seen and unseen
from the harsh whipstrokes of slavery
tortured and magnificent
proud and mysterious
Africa from head to foot
This is what I am.

If you want to understand me
come, bend over this soul of Africa
in the black dockworker's groans
the Chope's frenzied dances
the Changanas' rebellion
in the strange sadness which flows
from an African song, through the night.

And ask no more
to know me
for I'm nothing but a shell of flesh
where Africa's revolt congealed
its cry pregnant with hope.

The Poem of Joao

Joao was young like us
Joao had wideawake eyes
and alert ears
hands reaching forwards
a mind cast for tomorrow
a mouth to cry an eternal 'no'
Joao was young like us.

Joao enjoyed art and literature
enjoyed poetry and Jorge Amado
enjoyed books of meat and soul
which breathe life, struggle, sweat and hope
Joao dreamt of Zambesi's flowing books spreading culture
for mankind, for the young, our brothers
Joao fought that books might be for all
Joao loved literature
Joao was young like us.

Joao was the father, the mother, the brother of multitudes
Joao was the blood and the sweat of multitudes
and suffered and was happy like the multitudes
He smiled that same tired smile of shop girls leaving work
he suffered with the passivity of the peasant women
he felt the sun piercing like a thorn in the Arabs' midday
he bargained on bazaar benches with the Chinese
he sold tired green vegetables with the Asian traders
he howled spirituals from Harlem with Marion Anderson
he swayed to the Chope marimbas on a Sunday
he cried out with the rebels their cry of blood
he was happy in the caress of the manioc-white moon
he sang with the shibalos their songs of homesick longing
and he hoped with the same intensity of all
for dazzling dawns with open mouths
to sing
Joao was the blood and sweat of multitudes
Joao was young like us.

Joao and Mozambique were intermingled
Joao would not have been Joao without Mozambique
Joao was like a palm tree, a coconut palm
a piece of rock, a Lake Niassa, a mountain
an Incomati, a forest, a macala tree
a beach, a Maputo, an Indian Ocean
Joao was an integral and deep rooted part of Mozambique
Joao was young like us.

Joao longed to live and longed to conquer life
that is why he loathed prisons, cages, bars
and loathed the men who make them.
For Joao was free
Joao was an eagle born to fly
Joao loathed prisons and the men who make them
Joao was young like us.

And because Joao was young like us
and had wide awake eyes
ane enjoyed art and poetry and Jorge Amado
and was the blood and sweat of multitudes
and was intermingled with Mozambique

and was an eagle born to fly
and hated prisons and the men who make them
Ah, because of all this we have lost Joao
We have lost Joao.

Ah, this is why we have lost Joao
why we weep night and day for Joao
for Joao whom they have stolen from us.

And we ask
But why have they taken Joao,
Joao who was young and ardent like us
Joao who thirsted for life
Joao who was brother to us all
why have they stolen from us Joao
who spoke of hope and dawning days
Joao whose glance was like a brother's hug
Joao who always had somewhere for one of us to stay
Joao who was our mother and our father
Joao who would have been our saviour
Joao whom we loved and love
Joao who belongs so surely to us
oh, why have they stolen Joao from us?
and no one answers
indifferent, no one answers.

But we know
why they took Joao from us
Joao, so truly our brother.

But what does it matter?
They think they have stolen him but Joao is here with us
is here in others who will come
in others who have come.
For Joao is not alone
Joao is a multitude
Joao is the blood and the sweat of multitudes
and Joao, in being Joao, is also Joaquim, José,
Abdullah, Fang, Mussumbuluco, is Mascarenhas
Omar, Yutang, Fabiao,
Joao is the multitude, the blood and sweat of multitudes.

And who will take José, Joaquim, Abdullah,
Fang, Mussumbuluco, Mascarenhas, Omar, Fabiao?
Who?
Who will take us all and lock us in a cage?
Ah, they have stolen Joao from us
But Joao is us all.
Because of this Joao hasn't left us
and Joao 'was' not, he 'is' and 'will be'.

For Joao is us all, we are a multitude
and the multitude
who can take the multitude and lock it in a cage?

Agostinho Neto

Kinaxixi

I was glad to sit down
on a bench in Kinaxixi
at six o'clock of a hot evening
and just sit there . . .

Someone would come
maybe
to sit beside me

And I would see the black faces
of the people going uptown
in no hurry
expressing absence in the
jumbled Kimbundu they conversed in.

I would see the tired footsteps
of the servants whose fathers also are servants
looking for love here, glory there, wanting
something more than drunkenness in every
alcohol

Neither happiness nor hate

After the sun had set
lights would be turned on and I
would wander off
thinking that our life after all is simple
too simple
for anyone who is tired and still has to walk.

Western Civilisation

Sheets of tin nailed to posts
driven in the ground
make up the house.

Some rags complete
the intimate landscape.

The sun slanting through cracks
welcomes the owner

After twelve hours of slave
labour.

breaking rock
shifting rock
breaking rock
shifting rock
fair weather
wet weather
breaking rock
shifting rock

Old age comes early

a mat on dark nights
is enough when he dies
gratefully
of hunger.

Hoisting the Flag

When I returned
the soldier ants had vanished from the town
And you too
My friend Liceu
voice gladdening with hot rhythms of the land
through nights of never-failing Saturdays,
You too
sacred and ancestral music
resurgent in the sacred sway of the Ngola's rhythm,
You too had vanished
and with you
the intellectuals
the Ligue
Farolim
the Ingombata meetings
the conscience of traitors betraying without love.
I came just at the moment of the dawning cataclysm
as the seedling bursts the rain damped ground
thrusting up resplendent in youth and colour,
I came to see the resurrection of the seed,
the dynamic symphony of joy growing among men.
And the blood and the suffering
was a tempestuous flood which split the town.

When I came back
the day had been chosen
and the hour was at hand.

Even the children's laughter had gone
and you too
my good friends, my brothers,
Benge, Joaquim, Gaspar, Ilidio, Manuel

and who else?
hundreds, thousands of you, my friends
some for ever vanished,
ever victorious in their death for life.

When I came back
some momentous thing was moving in the land
the granary guards kept closer watch,
the school children studied harder
the sun shone brighter,
there was a youthful calm among the old people,
more than hope—it was certainty
more than goodness—it was love.

Men's strength
soldiers' courage
poets' cries
were all trying to raise up
beyond the memory of heroes.
Ngola Kiluanji,
Rainha Jinga,
trying to raise up high
the flag of independence.

José Craveirinha

Mamparra M'gaiza*

The cattle is selected
counted, marked
and gets on the train, stupid cattle.

In the pen
the females stay behind
to breed new cattle.

The train is back from 'migoudini'**
and they come rotten with diseases, the old cattle of Africa
oh, and they've lost their heads, these cattle 'm'gaiza'.

Come and see
the sold cattle have lost their heads
my god of my land
the sold cattle have lost their heads.

Again
the cattle is selected, marked
and the train is ready to take away meek cattle

Stupid cattle
mine cattle
cattle of Africa, marked and sold.

*M'gaiza (also magaica) is a Mozambiquan expression for a man just
    returned from the mines, his pockets full of money and his health
    broken.
**Dialect for the mines.

Mamana Saquina

Mamana Saquina
in the cosmopolitan, the dazzling mirage of the town
still kept her magic charms within her heart
at the hour of mourning
Joao.

Mamana Saquina
still kept the train's image in her mind
tangled with a song of steel on steel
to the beat Joao-Tavasse-went-to-the-mines
Joao-Tavasse-went-to-the-mines
Joao-Tavasse-went-to-the-mines

Joao-Tavasse-went-to-the-mines
Joao-Tavasse-went-to-the-mines

(On that morning of gilded cashew leaves
Joao Tavasse went to sign up at the depot)

And Mamana Saquina
stayed at Chibuto on the land
with Mamana Rosalina and cocuana Massingue
with ten hectares
in which to sow and bring to flower
the concession's seed

Night and day
the soul of Mamana Saquina swathed itself in nightmare
and buried itself in ten hectares of flowering cotton
(And Joao Tavasse
never came back to the depot)

Belching steam the miners' train pulled out
and in the pistons a voice sang
Joao-Tavasse-went-to-the-mines
Joao-Tavasse-went-to-the-mines
Joao-Tavasse-went-to-the-mines
Joao-Tavasse-went-to-the-mines

And Mamana Saquina mourned her son
scratched maize from the ground
and achieved the miracle of one hundred and fifty
five bales of cotton.

Arnaldo Santos

The Return

Colourless banners
Trembling in the wind

A truck passes and voices sing
  —men going home

The full song carries far
To scattered huts where mothers wait

Banner-desires
Trembling in the wind

And voices left traced on the matting floor
Like the dust of the streets
Their songs of parting

And ever trembling
Colourless banners arouse desires

In the townships, new babies' cries are formed.

Costa Andrade

Fourth Poem

There are on the earth 50,000 dead whom no one
   mourned
      on the earth
        unburied
           50,000 dead
whom no one mourned

A thousand Guernicas and the message in the
   brush-strokes of Orozco and
        de Siqueiros

it had the dimensions of the sea, this silence
spread across the land

        as if the rains rained blood
        as if the coarse hair was grass many metres high
        as if the mouths condemned
        in the very moment of their 50,000 deaths
        all the living of the earth

There are on the earth 50,000 dead
whom no one mourned

no one . . .

the mothers of Angola
        died together with their sons.

Rui de Matos

Geology Lesson

Earth is an amalgam
of sands, humus and clays.
Earth is a mixture
of sticks, bones and waste.

Earth is made of blood,
of ores,
of sweat and phlegm of slaves.

Earth is made of pain,
of mineral salts
of misery and roots.

Earth is made of rocks
and gnashing teeth.

Earth is an amalgam
of hatreds stone and love,
of clay and iron hopes.

Earth is the place of deserts,
plains, mountains and the sea.

Earth is the place of man.

Earth is the place of men
who make it free
to be free.

Earth is made of land
by folk from the land itself.

Jorge Rebelo

Poem

Come, brother and tell me your life
come, show me the marks of revolt
        which the enemy left on your body

Come, say to me 'Here
my hands have been crushed
because they defended
the land which they own

'Here my body was tortured
because it refused to bend
to invaders

'Here my mouth was wounded
because it dared to sing
my people's freedom'

Come brother and tell me your life,
come relate me the dreams of revolt
which you and your fathers and forefathers
dreamed
in silence
through shadowless nights made for love

Come tell me these dreams become
war,
the birth of heroes,
land reconquered,
mothers who, fearless,
send their sons to fight.

Come, tell me all this, my brother.

And later I will forge simple words
which even the children can understand
words which will enter every house
like wind
and fall like red hot embers
on our people's souls.

In our land
Bullets are beginning to flower.

Biographical Notes

Abrahams, Peter Born 1919 in Vrededorp. Left South Africa for England in 1939 and moved to Jamaica in 1955. Journalist, broadcaster; has published numerous novels and a collection of poetry, *A Blackman Speaks of Freedom!* (1940).

Andrade, Costa Born 1936 in Lépi, Angola. Has lived in Italy, Brazil and Portugal. Served with the MPLA forces and was in 1976 appointed Director of the *Jornal de Angola*, the main daily newspaper in Luanda. Publications include *O Regresso e o Canto* (1975), *Poesia com Armas* (1975) and *O Caderno dos Heróis* (1977).

Banana, Canaan President of Zimbabwe.

Banoobhai, Shabbir Born 1949 in Durban. Lecturer in Accountancy at the University of Durban-Westville. Poetry publications: *echoes of my other self* (1980) and *shadows of a sun-darkened land* (1984).

Brand, Dollar (Abdullah Ibrahim) Born in Cape Town. Has travelled Europe and USA as Afro-jazz musician. Poems in *The Classic* and in Cosmo Pieterse's *Seven South African Poets* (1970).

Chimsoro, Samuel Contemporary Zimbabwean poet whose single collection is *Smoke and Flames* (1978).

Craveirinha, José Born 1922 in Maputo, Mozambique. Journalist, poet and was active in FRELIMO. Publication: *Chigubo*.

Dangor, Achmat Born in 1948 in Johannesburg. Manager in an international company in Johannesburg. Banned 1973-'78. Editor; Mofolo-Plomer Prize for stories published as *Waiting for Leila* (1981). Poetry in *Wietie, Staffrider, A Century of South African Poetry* (1981) and in his own volume *Bulldozer* (1983).

Davids, Jennifer Born 1945 in Cape Town. Schoolteacher in London and Cape Town. Poetry publication: *Searching for Words* (1974).

Dhlomo, Herbert Isaac Ernest (1903 - 1956). Born in Natal. Teacher, journalist on *Bantu World,* assistant editor on *Ilanga Lase Natal.* Librarian-Organiser for the Carnegie Library in Germiston and was responsible for establishing library facilities for blacks throughout the Transvaal. Wrote plays, numerous critical articles on African poetry and drama, as well as the long poem *Valley of a Thousand Hills* (1941). His *Collected Works* appeared in 1985.

Dube, Mrs. A.C. Relative of John Dube, first President of the ANC and founder of *Ilanga Lase Natal.*

Gwala, Mafika Born 1946 in Natal. Has worked as a legal clerk, teacher, factory-hand and publications researcher. Edited *Black Review* (1973) and has contributed critical articles on contemporary black South African literature. Poetry publications: *Jol'iinkomo* (1977) and *No More Lullabies* (1982).

Jiggs, pen-name of Colin Smuts. Born 1944 in Johannesburg. Directs the creative arts programme for the Open School in Doornfontein.

Johennesse, Fhazel Born 1956 in Johannesburg. Co-director of Sable Books and *Wietie* magazine. Poetry publication: *The Rainmaker* (1979).

Jolobe, James James Ranisi (1902 - 1976). Born Cape Province. Schoolteacher, minister of religion, essayist, novelist, playwright, translator. Helped compose the Xhosa-English-Afrikaans dictionary. Received the 1952 Vilakazi Memorial Prize for Literature and an honorary degree from the University of Fort Hare in 1974. Poetry publications include *Umyezo* (1936) and *Ilitha* (1959) in Xhosa and *Poems of an African* (1946), his own transalations from *Umyezo.*

Langa, Mandlenkosi Now living in Gaborone where he helped found the Medu Art Ensemble. Poetry in *To Whom It May Concern: An Anthology of Black South African Poetry* (1973).

L.R. Pen-name, during the 1930s, of a staff-writer on the newspaper *Umteteli wa Bantu.*

Madingoane, Ingoapele Oral delivery of his epic poem 'black trial' (published as *Africa My Beginning,* in 1979) played a part in reviving a context of poetry performance at the time of the 1976 events in Soweto.

Matos, Rui de Born 1943 in Luanda. Commander in the MPLA forces. Sculptor and one of the new generation of 'warrior poets' first published by the MPLA's department of education and culture.

Matthews, James Born 1929 in Athlone. Journalist and Director of Blac Publishing House. Political detainee for four months in 1976/77. Short-story writer, editor of *Black Voices Shout: An Anthology of Poetry* (1974). Poetry publications: (with Gladys Thomas) *Cry Rage!* (1972), *Pass Me a Meatball, Jones* (1977; banned) and *no time for dreams* (1981).

Motjuwadi, Stanley Editor of *Drum*, his poetry has appeared in the anthology *To Whom It May Concern*.

Motshile, Nthodi wa Born 1948 near Pretoria. Has exhibited graphic art widely in South Africa and is studying abroad. Poetry publication: *From the Calabash: Poems and Woodcuts* (1978).

Motsisi, Moses Karabo (Casey) (1932 - 1977). Short-story writer, journalist on *Drum*, known as 'The Kid'. Poem in *The Classic;* writings collected in *Casey & Co.* (1978).

Mphahlele, Es'kia (Ezekiel) Born in 1919. Went into exile as a result of his opposition to Bantu Education and held senior academic posts in Africa and USA before returning to South Africa in 1979. Currently a Professor in the African Studies Institute, University of the Witwatersrand, he has published novels *(Down Second Avenue* and *Chirundu)*, short stories and critical works *(The African Image* and *Voices in the Whirlwind)*. Some of his shorter writings, including his poetry, collected in *The Unbroken Song* (1981).

Mqhayi, Samuel Edward Krune (1875 - 1945). Born Tyume Valley, Gqumahashe. Educated at Lovedale where he was later a lecturer. Active in politics and journalism; editor of the newspaer *Imvo Zabantsundu*. Adviser on Xhosa grammar and usage. Wrote novels, biographies and essays and published three volumes of poetry including *Inzuzo*. Recognised as famous imbongi. Considered the greatest Xhosa poet and referred to as 'The Poet of our Race'.

Mtshali, Mbuyiseni Oswald Born 1940 in Vryheid, Natal. Has worked as a messenger, later arts critic and currently vice-principal of a Soweto college. Awarded the 1974 Olive Schreiner Prize for his first collection *Sounds of a Cowhide Drum* (1971). On his return from Columbia University, his second collection, *Fireflames*, was published in 1980.

Mungoshi, Charles Born 1947 near Enkeldoorn. On editorial staff of the Zimbabwe Literature Bureau. Novel, *Waiting for the Rain*, won a 1976 Pen Award. Poetry in *Staffrider* and in the anthology *Zimbabwe Poetry in English* (1978).

Mutloatse, Mothobi Journalist on *The Voice;* editor of *Casey & Co.* (1978) and *Forced Landing: Contemporary Black Prose Writing from Africa South* (1980). Poetry in *Staffrider*.

Ndebele, Njabulo S. Lecturer in Literature at the University of Lesotho and currently researching in USA. Has contributed critical work on black South African poetry; poems in periodicals and in the anthologies *To Whom It May Concern* and *A Century of South African Poetry.*

Neto, Agostinho (1922 - 1979). Born in the Catete region of Angola, he studied medicine in Lisbon and Coimbra. Medical practice in Luanda became a cover for his MPLA activities. Periodically detained by the Portuguese colonial authorities, he was at the time of his death President of independent Angola. A prolific poet, his last collection was *Segrada Esperanca* (1974), *Sacred Hope,* English edition (1974).

Nhlapo, Walter M.B. Past editor of *Bantu World.*

Patel, Essop Trained as an attorney and lives in Johannesburg. Edited collected writings *The World of Nat Nakasa* (1975). Poetry publication: *They Came at Dawn* (1980).

Pote, Henry Born 1939 near Ndanga Hospital, Zimbabwe. Educated at Gokomere Mission and Roma University. Formerly a teacher, he has written in Shona and English.

Rebelo, Jorge Born 1940 in Maputo. Educated at Coimbra University. FRELIMO Secretary for Information and edits the magazine *Mozambique Revolution.*

Santos, Arnaldo Born 1936 in Luanda. Civil servant and one-time clandestine MPLA organiser. Short-story writer and poet whose publications include *Fuga* and *Quinaxixe.*

Sepamla, Sipho Born 1939 in Krugersdorp. Director of the Federated Union of Black Arts (FUBA). Joint recipient of the 1976 Pringle Award. He has written short stories and novels. Poetry publications: *Hurry Up To It!* (1975), *The Blues Is You in Me* (1976), *The Soweto I Love* (1977), *Children of the Earth* (1983) and *Selected Poems* (1984).

Serote, Mongane Wally Born 1944 in Sophiatown. In political detention for nine months in 1969. Received the Ingrid Jonker Prize for Poetry in 1973. Has lived in self-imposed exile in Gaborone and now in Britain. Has written articles, short stories and a novel. Poetry publications: *Yakhal'inkomo* (1972), *Tsetlo* (1974), *No Baby Must Weep* (1975), *Behold Mama, Flowers* (1978) and *Selected Poems* (1982).

Soga, Allan Kirkland Journalist and son of the famous Tiyo Soga, and editor of *Izwe la Bantu.* Occasional poems appeared in the late nineteenth century.

Sousa, Noemia de Born 1927 in Maputo.

Van Wyk, Christopher Born 1957 in Johannesburg. Co-director of Sable Books and *Wietie* magazine. Has written short stories and is joint recipient of the 1980 Olive Schreiner Prize for his first collection of poetry, *It Is Time to Go Home* (1979).

Vilakazi, Benedict Wallet (1906 - 1947). Born in Groutville, Natal. Educated at the University of the Witwatersrand where he later lectured in African studies. Linguistic authority and joint compiler of the standard Zulu-English dictionary. Memorial Vilakazi Award was established for Nguni Literature. Poetry publications: *Inkondlo kaZulu* and *Amal'ezulu* and translated into English in *Zulu Horizons* (1975).

Yako, St J. Page Xhosa poet and teacher. Poetry publications: *Umtha Welanga* and *Ikwesi* and poems translated in the Xhosa-to-English anthology *The Making of a Servant & Other Poems* (1972).

Zimunya, Musaemura (Bonus) Born in Umtali. Left what was then Rhodesia in 1975 following imprisonment after a demonstration. Studied at university abroad and is currently a research fellow at the University of Zimbabwe. Co-editor of the anthology *And Now the Poets Speak: Poems Inspired by the Struggle for Zimbabwe* (1981). Poetry in *Chirimo, Staffrider*, the anthology *A Century of South African Poetry* and collected in *Zimbabwe Ruins* (1979).

Acknowledgements

Although every effort has been made to trace the copyright holders this has not always been possible. Should any infringement have occurred the publisher apologises and undertakes to amend the omission in the event of a reprint.

The editor and publisher gratefully acknowledge the following copyright holders:

Peter Abrahams ('Self'; 'For Laughter'; 'Freedom's Child', from *A Blackman Speaks of Freedom!*) **Costa Andrade** and East African Publishing House ('The Return', tr. Margaret Dickinson, from *Where Bullets Begin to Flower*) **Anonymous** poem 'Shantytown, from *Inkululiko* **Farouk Asvat** ('Possibilities for a Man Hunted by SBs', from *Staffrider*) **Canaan Banana** and Mambo Press ('Liberating Love' from *And Now the Poets Speak*) **Shabbir Banoobhai** and Ravan Press ('the morning caught me'; 'the border'; 'for my father', from *echoes of my other self*) **D.G.T. Bereng** (estate) ('Litholhokiso tsa Moshoeshoe', tr. D. Kunene as 'The Birth of Moshesh', from *The Penguin Book of South African Verse*) **Dollar Brand** (extract 'Africa, Music and Show Business' from *The Classic*) **Paul Chidyausiku** and Ad. Donker ('Grandpa' from *A Century of South African Poetry*) **Samuel Chimsoro** and Mambo Press ('Basket and Stones'; The Curfew Breakers'; 'The Change'; 'I Love', from *Smoke and Flames*) **Julius Chingono** ('To You Father'; 'Thank Thee Mother'; 'Big Boys Don't Cry', from *Quarry*) **Shimmer Chinodya** and Mambo Press ('Recollections' from *Zimbabwean Poetry in English*) **Chirwa P. Chipeya** ('change'; 'today the war has ended', from *Staffrider*) **José Craveirinha** and East African Publishing House ('Mamparra M'gaiza'; 'Mamana Saquina', tr. Margaret Dickinson, from *Where Bullets Begin to Flower*) **Achmat Dangor** and Ad. Donker ('The Voices that are Dead' from *A Century of South African Poetry*) **Jennifer Davids** and David Philip ('Searching for Words'; 'Location Fires'; 'Poem for my Mother', from *Searching for Words*) **Rui de Matos** and Heinemann ('Geology Lesson', tr. M. Wolfers, from *Poems from Angola*) **Noemia de Sousa** and East African Publishing House ('If You Want to Know Me'; 'The Poem of Joao', tr. Margaret Dickinson, from *Where Bullets Begin to Flower*) **H.I.E. Dhlomo** (estate) ('Because I'm Black'; 'The Question (Beasts or Broth-

ers)'; 'Not for Me'); Knox Printers (extract from *Valley of a Thousand Hills)*
Enver Docratt (estate) ('The Storm'; 'The Slender Child', from *The Classic)*
Mrs. A.C. Dube (estate) and Ravan Press ('Africa : My Native Land' from
Reconstruction) **Mike Dues** ('Armies of the Night' from *New Nation;*
'Hunger Wrote the Epitaph' from *Staffrider)* **Godfrey Dzvairo** and Mambo
Press ('Follow my Mind' from *And Now the Poets Speak)* **S.C. Faber** (estate)
('The Scolly' from *Cape Standard)* **Mafika Gwala** and Ad.Donker ('Kwela-
Ride'; 'One Small Boy Longs for Summer'; 'We Lie under Tall Gum Trees';
'The Bangalala'; 'Night Party'; 'The Children of Nonti'; 'Food for the Couple';
'Getting off the Ride', from *Jol'ünkomo)* **Indigenous** Work Song ('Pass
Office Song' transcribed Peggy Rutherford) **Jiggs** (Colin Smuts) and Ad.
Donker ('Doornfontein' from *A Century of South African Poetry)* **Fhazel
Johennesse** and Ravan Press ('the african pot'; 'for george masoka'; 'the taxi
driver'; 'thinking about a white christmas'; 'my township sunset', from *The
Rainmaker)* **J.J.R. Jolobe** (estate), Witwatersrand University Press and
Ophir ('Ukwenziwa komkhonzi' from *Umyezo,* tr. R. Kavanagh &
Z. Quangule as 'The Making of a Servant' from *The Making of a Servant)*
Mandlenkosi Langa and Ad. Donker ('The Pension Jiveass' from *To Whom It
May Concern)* **786/Monnapule Lebakeng** ('The Dying Ground' from *Staff-
rider)* **L.R.** (' "Civilised" Labour Policy' from *Umteleli wa Bantu)* **Ingoapele
Madingoane** and Ravan Press (extract from 'black trial', from *Africa my
Beginning)* **Albert G.T.K. Malikongwa** ('A Protest from a Bushman' from
Staffrider) **Senzo Malinga** ('At War with the Preacherman' from *Staffrider)*
Bicca Maseko and Ad. Donker ('King Mzilikazi Revisited' from *A Century of
South African Poetry)* **James Matthews** and Spro-Cas/Ravan ('It Is Said' from
Cry Rage!); Blac ('women of dimbaza and ilinge' from *Black Voices Shout!)*
Mafika Mbuli and Ad. Donker ('The Miners' from *To Whom It May Concern)*
M.G. (estate) ('Black and White' from *Bantu World)* **Richard Mhonyera** and
Mambo Press ('Rhodes' from *Zimbabwean Poetry in English)* **Themba ka
Miya** ('The Question' from *New Classic)* **Molahlehi wa Mmutle** ('Our Immor-
tal Mother' from *Staffrider)* **Nkathazo ka Mnyayiza** ('Bad Friday'; 'Kneel and
Pray', from *Ophir;* 'Forgotten People' from *Staffrider)* **Stanley Mogoba** and
Ad. Donker ('Cement' from *To Whom It May Concern)* **Motlase Mogotsi**
('Soul's Disparity'; 'The Unforgettable Mistake', from *Staffrider)* **David Moja-
Mphuso** ('Old Homes' from *Staffrider)* **Zulu Molefe** ('To Paint a Black
Woman' from *Contrast);* Ad. Donker ('Black Zionist Meeting' from *To Whom
It May Concern)* **Nape 'a Motana** ('Village from the Portion of my Mind'
from *Staffrider)* **Stanley Motjuwadi** and Ad. Donker ('White Lies' from *To
Whom It May Concern)* **Casey Motsisi** (estate) and Ad. Donker ('The
Efficacy of Prayer' from *To Whom It May Concern)* **Es'kia Mphahlele** and
Ravan Press ('Death'; 'Somewhere'; 'Fathers and Sons', from *The Unbroken
Song)* **Daizer Mqhaba** ('Tshisa-Nyama' from *Staffrider)* **S.E.K. Mqhayi**

(estate), Witwatersrand University Press & Ophir ('Itshawe lase Bhritani' from *Imzuzo;* tr. R. Kavanagh & Z. Quangule as 'The Prince of Britain', from *The Making of a Servant)* **J.I. Msikinya** (estate) ('Africa's Tears' from *Koranta a Beccana)* **Oupa Thando Mthimkulu** ('Nineteen Seventy-Six' from *Staffrider)* **Mbuyiseni Oswald Mtshali** and Ad. Donker ('Boy on a Swing'; 'Always a Suspect'; 'An Abandoned Bundle'; 'The Detribalised', from *Sounds of a Cowhide Drum);* Shuter & Shooter ('Talismans'; 'Weep Not for a Warrior', from *Fireflames)* **Kizito Muchemwa** and Mambo Press ('Tourists' from *Zimbabwean Poetry in English)* **Charles Mungoshi** ('Burning Log' from *Staffrider);* Mambo Press ('If You Don't Stay Bitter and Angry for Too Long'; 'Mwari Komborerai', from *And Now the Poets Speak)* **Mothobi Mutloatse** ('Mamellang' from *New Nation);* Ad. Donker ('Ngwana wa Azania' from *A Century of South African Poetry)* **Rev. Pambari Jeremiah Mzimba** (estate) and Ravan Press ('It Walks' from *Reconstruction)* **Njabulo S. Ndebele** ('Five Letters to M.M.M.' from *Expression);* Ad. Donker ('The Man of Smoke'; 'I Hid my Love', from *To Whom It May Concern)* **Mandla Ndlozi** ('A Visit to Isandhlawana' from *Staffrider)* **Agostinho Neto** (estate) and East African Publishing House ('Kinaxixi'; 'Western Civilisation'; 'Hoisting the Flag', tr. Margaret Dickinson, from *Where Bullets Begin to Flower)* **Walter M.B. Nhlapo** (estate) ('The Revolution Song' from *Bantu World;* 'Tomorrow' from *The Voice of Africa)* **C.D. Noble** ('Who Is the Rain?' from *New Classic);* **Motshile wa Nthodi** ('Standard Fifty-Eight' from *New Classic);* Ad. Donker ('South African Dialogue' from *A Century of South African Poetry)* **Pathisa Nyathi** and Mambo Press ('Till Silence Be Broken' from *And Now the Poets Speak)* **Essop Patel** and Blac ('On the Steps'; 'Barbed Wire Silence'; 'Baby Thembisa'; 'Houghton Party/Saturday Night Sunday Morning Poem'; 'They Came at Dawn', from *They Came at Dawn)* **Nthambeleni Phalanndwa** and Ravan Press ('In This World my Sister' from *Reconstruction)* **Kriben Pillay** ('A Letter to Bandi' from *Staffrider)* **Henry Pote** and Mambo Press ('To my Elders' from *Zimbabwean Poetry in English)* **Jorge Rebelo** and East African Publishing House ('Poem', tr. Margaret Dickinson, from *Where Bullets Begin to Flower)* **Arnaldo Santos** and East African Publishing House ('The Return', tr. Margaret Dickinson, from *Where Bullets Begin to Flower)* **Demetrius Segooa** (estate) ('Praises of the Train, recorded H.J. van Zyl, from *The Penguin Book of South African Verse)* **Magoleng wa Selepe** and Ad. Donker ('My Name' from *A Century of South African Poetry)* **Sipho Sepamla** and Ad. Donker ('To Whom It May Concern'; 'Come Duze Baby', from *Hurry Up to It;* 'The Blues Is You in Me'; 'I Tried to Say'; 'Double-Talk'; 'Statement: The Dodger'; 'Song of Mother and Child', from *The Blues Is You in Me);* Rex Collings & David Philip ('Soweto' from *The Soweto I Love)* **Mongane W. Serote** and Ad. Donker ('Alexandra'; 'City Johannesburg'; 'A Poem'; 'What's in This Black "Shit" ', from *Yakhal'inkomo;* 'A Poem on Black and White';

'Death Survey'; 'Introit', from *Tsetlo;* extract from *No Baby Must Weep;* 'Child of the Song' from *Behold Mama, Flowers;* 'Time Has Run Out' from *Selected Poems)* **Eugene Skeef** ('We the Dancers' from *Staffrider)* **A.K. Soga** (estate)('Santa Cruz : The Holy Cross' from *Imvo Zabantsuṇdu);* Ravan Press ('Ntsikana's Vision' from *Reconstruction* **Basil Somhahlo** and Ad. Donker ('Who Wants to be Mothered?' from *To Whom It May Concern)* **Farouk Stemmet** ('Custodian of our Spirit' from *Staffrider)* **Traditional** Jack Cope (Prayer to the Hunting Star, Canopus'; 'The Wind and the Bird'; 'Hymn to Tsui-Xgoa'; 'How Death Came'; Lament for a Warrior'; 'Praises of the King Tshaka'; 'Ngoni Burial Song'; 'Love is Bitter', from *The Penguin Book of South African Verse)* **Christopher van Wyk** and Ad. Donker ('metamorphosis'; 'Injustice'; 'About Graffiti'; 'Me and the Rain'; 'Beware of White Ladies when the Spring is Here'; 'Confession'; 'Catharsis'; 'A Riot Policeman'; 'Candle', from *It is Time to Go Home)* **B.W. Vilakazi** (estate) and Witwatersrand University Press (I Hear a Singing'; 'The Gold Mines', lit. tr. D.McK Malcolm & J. Sikakana, into verse Florence L. Friedman from *Zulu Horizons)* **St. J. Page Yako,** Afrikaanse Pers & Ophir ('Ukufinyenzwa mokubiywa komhlaba' from *Umtha welanga,* tr. R. Kavanagh & Z. Quangule as 'The Contraction and Enclosure of the Land' in *The Making of a Servant* **Musaemura Zimunya** and The Poetry Society of Rhodesia ('No Songs'; 'Efulamachina'; 'Roads'; 'Chimpanzee'; 'White Padre'; 'The Reason'; 'Rooster'; from *Zimbabwe Ruins);* Mambo Press ('After the Massacre' from *And Now the Poets Speak)* **Eddison Zvobgo** and Mambo Press ('My Companion and Friend : The Bare Brick in my Prison Cell' from *And Now the Poets Speak)* **K. Zwide** ('Wooden Spoon' from *Staffrider).*

Index of Poets

Michael Chapman and Tony Voss

ACCENTS

An anthology of poetry from the English-speaking world

Accents, compiled by Tony Voss and Mike Chapman, of the University of Natal, is an introductory anthology of poetry, with a difference. The selection is aimed primarily at first-year university and college students, but also at general readers who, through this book, may acquaint themselves with the vast range of English poetry from the Middle Ages to the present day. The volume includes poems of the 'old favourites' such as Shakespeare, Wordsworth, Tennyson, Milton, Yeats, Shelley and Keats; as well as selected South African poetry, from Thomas Pringle to the Soweto poets, including some examples of African oral poetry; and poems of modern British and American poets such as e.e. cummings and Ezra Pound.

255 pages, a paperbook

Michael Chapman

THE PAPERBOOK OF
SOUTH AFRICAN ENGLISH POETRY

This anthology offers a selection of South African poetry
written in English, from its beginnings in the 1820s to the
mid-1980s. *The Paperbook* attempts to bring to the reader
fresh examples of our poetry, and to indicate something of
the developments over the last few years, but also includes
the 'significant markers' within the landscape of South African English poetry, such as Pringle's 'Afar in the Desert',
Campbell's 'The Zulu Girl', and Serote's 'City Johannesburg'.
Over one hundred poets are represented, more or less in the
order in which they first came to prominence. The compila-
tion includes a detailed introduction, biographical notes
with brief explanatory comments on some of the poems,
and a select bibliography of critical material.

320 pages, a paperbook

Sisa Ndaba

ONE DAY IN JUNE

Poetry and prose from troubled times

One Day in June is a documentary of outrage and passion in poetry and prose spanning the ten years from 1976. Its only theme is the pain and suffering that black people experienced and are experiencing. The anthology includes articles by people such as Black Consciousness leader Steve Biko, Allan Boesak and Mafika Gwala; and poems by Mbuyiseni Oswald Mtshali, Sipho Sepamla, Mongane Wally Serote, James Matthews and others.

128 pages, a paperbook